Skip·Beat!

Skip·Beat!

Volume 25

CONTENTS

Skip·Beat!
Act 145: Valentine Bug

I THOUGHT ...

...ON VALENTINE'S DAY...

...YOUR HEART ONLY FLUT-TERED ...

...WHEN YOU GAVE YOUR GUY CHOCO-LATES.

KYOKO...
YES?
LOOK...
HUH?
IF...

...HE...
...HADN'T SHOWN UP TODAY...

...
DID HE...
whisper
...COME TO SEE KYOKO?
I guess...
TO RECEIVE... THOSE CHOCO-LATES?!
YOU DO IT WHERE REN ISN'T!
How could you have him come HERE?!
HATE
That's why he brought those flowers, as a thank-you gift?!
Ugh, no...
KYOKO...
How could you?!

tmp

YOU LOOK ...
...REAL STUPID...
TH...
That's because you look so out of place here!
What the hell are you doing here?!
Are you working part-time for a florist?!
Or is this for a TV show?!
...
WHAT ...
...DO YOU ...
... THINK OF THIS?
rustle
HUH ?

Sparkling beads
Phalaenopsis orchids
Swa●vski
Freshwater pearls
.....
It's ...
It's pretty※ ...
RIGHT?
IT LOOKS EXPENSIVE...
THE DECORATION LOOKS MORE EXPENSIVE THAN THE FLOWERS ...
THIS IS ALL STUFF THAT I THOUGHT YOU LIKE...
※ She can't help saying it.

...SO OF COURSE YOU LOVE IT.
?!
Wha...
WHY'D YOU GET SOME-THING I'D LIKE—
AND SO.
TOSS
Huh?!
!
WHAP
Wah!
?!
IT'S FOR YOU.
CONGRAT-ULATIONS.
Uh
TH...
THIS IS HEAVY!
?!

CONGRATU-
LATIONS?
UH...
WHAT?
I'VE KNOWN YOU FOR A LONG TIME...
...AND ONLY I KNOW THAT YOU'VE NEVER GONE OUT WITH A GUY, NOT EVEN ONCE.
I'M THE ONLY ONE WHO CAN CONGRAT-
ULATE YOU...
...SO, I'M DOING IT AS A CHILDHOOD FRIEND.

SO CONGRATS ON GOING OUT WITH VIE GHOUL'S VOCALIST.

WHAT ?!

WHAT THE HECK?!

WH...

KYOKO ...

You're going out with VIE GHOUL's vocalist?!
No!
Wow!
Mysterious♡ Beautiful♡ He may not be hu~ma~n♡
People's comments (Girls only)
How'd you get to know someone like him?!
Did you get to know him through Sho?!
I'M NOT GOING OUT WITH HIM!
Ms. Momose and Ms. Ohara don't know about the stalker incident.
HEY, YOU!
ZAT
DOINK
WHY AM I GOING OUT WITH THE BEAGLE?!
Is this some sort of harassment?!
WHY'D YOU START ACTING LIKE THIS YESTERDAY?! YOU'VE BEEN TREATING ME LIKE A STUPID WOMAN WHO ONLY THINKS ABOUT LOVE!
Pisses me off!
HMM?
KYOKO SAW SHO YESTER-DAY...
...
Huh?
THEN SHE GAVE HIM THOSE CHOCOLATES YESTER-DAY...
Well...
YOU DESERVE IT.
To be treated like a stupid woman.
YOU KEPT RUNNING AWAY FROM HIM...
...BUT YOU MADE HIM CHOCOLATES THAT SAY "♡ TO BEAGLE."
♡ TO
How much do you like visual-kei guys?
SOOO!
You're still saying that!

flip
IT DIDN'T SAY "♡ TO BEAGLE"!
IT SAID...
...WHEN I PUT BACK THE PIECES THAT WERE OUT OF ORDER AND WERE REVERSED...
shuff
klik
klak
shuff
shuff
...THIS IS...
...WHAT IT SAID!
Ta-Dah!
H
YOU
E
HATE
GO
LL
TO
...THIS!
BANG
E TO Beagle?
?
What the heck?
AND...
!

HATE
H
HATE
GO

Do you understand?!
THIS IS THE CHOCOLATE I WAS FORCED TO MAKE, BECAUSE THE BEAGLE UNFORTUNATELY TOOK ADVANTAGE OF ME!
It's full of my hate!
THEY'RE CURSED CHOCOLATES THAT WILL SEND ANYBODY WHO EATS THEM TO HELL!
REMEMBER THIS UNTIL THE DAY YOU DIE, STUPID SHO!
If you call me a stupid woman again, I will stalk you until you're born again, and curse you!
DOINK

AH...
M...
MR. TSURUGA!
Darn it! What did I just do?!
MR. TSURUGA'S HERE!
Oh no!
He's staring at me with a blank look!
I GOT CARRIED AWAY AND CONFESSED THAT I MADE CHOCOLATES FOR THE BEAGLE!

EVEN IF THE BEAGLE TOOK ADVANTAGE OF ME...
EVEN IF I MADE CURSING CHOCOLATES...
I STILL YIELDED TO THE ENEMY!
W-WHAT SHOULD I DO?!
HE MUST BE TOTALLY APPALLED!
...
THOSE CHOCO-LATES...
...WERE FOR THE VIE GHOUL VOCAL-IST...
FOR VIE GHOUL'S VOCALIST... I'M CURIOUS WHY THINGS TURNED OUT THAT WAY...
...BUT THEY...
...WEREN'T FOR SHO...

Kyoko... really made those chocolates...

W-What a surprise...

...she must've been really angry...

To make those chocolates.

What happened between her and the VIE GHOUL vocalist?

I have no idea...

...But...

WH...

WHAT SHOULD I DO?!

I'M SO SCARED, I CAN'T LOOK AT MR. TSURUGA!

A COWARD?! A LOSER?! THE CENTER OF THE CHICKEN?!

Kyoko's idea of the most chicken of the chicken.

WHAT DOES HE THINK OF ME?

Aah...

NO. NO, MR. TSURUGA!

SOMETHING UNBE-LIEVABLE AND BIZARRE HAPPENED!

Aaaaah!

BUT HE WON'T BELIEVE IT EVEN IF I TELL HIM THE TRUTH!

CUZ CUZ POC

YOU POOR THING...

IF I TELL HIM THE TRUTH, HE'LL GET ANGRY AGAIN!
And he might think I'm totally nuts!
NO!
Why do I have to get scolded?! I'm the victim!
SHFF

WHAT?
SO YOU'RE JUST KYOKO...

I THOUGHT YOU FINALLY HAD A BOYFRIEND...

...BUT THIS IS THE TRUTH...

I GUESS...

...YOU'LL NEVER HAVE A BOYFRIEND, EVER...

You miserable thing...

So serious

Shut your mouth!

Don't say it so seriously!

I DON'T WANT A BOYFRIEND ANYWAY!

I REALIZED ONE'D JUST BE IN MY WAY.

Thanks to you-know-who!

I'LL BE STRONG, INTELLIGENT AND TOUGH, AND LIVE MY LIFE ALONE!

...
I HATE IT WHEN YOU PITY ME LIKE THIS!
WHY DON'T YOU JUST MAKE FUN OF ME LIKE ALWAYS?!
...
I CAN'T HELP IT.
You deserve to be pitied.
THE ONLY GUY YOU GAVE CHOCOLATES TO THIS VALENTINE'S DAY...
...WAS THE VIE GHOUL VOCALIST, WHO GOT THIS CREEPY CHOCOLATE.
HOW DARE YOU!
I GAVE CHOCOLATES TO SO MANY PEOPLE, THIS WAS MY BUSIEST YEAR!
THERE WERE ALMOST TEN DARK MOON PEOPLE!
DARK MOON PEOPLE?
Yes.
I GAVE SOME TO THOSE ACTRESSES OVER THERE TOO.
And to the Director.
...

?
...
WH...
WHAT?
DID YOU...
...GIVE THEM TO REN TSURUGA TOO?
Wha...?!
N...
NOT TO MR. TSURUGA.
CUZ...
I DIDN'T MAKE CHOCO-LATES FOR HIM...

DIDN'T MAKE...?
SO...
YOU MADE SOMETHING ELSE FOR HIM...
NOW HE KNOWS!
WHY DID HE HAVE TO ASK?!
MOKO DIDN'T ASK ME ABOUT IT!
...
WHAT'RE YOU GIVING HIM?
IT'S ...
IT'S NONE OF YOUR BUSINESS!
I don't need to tell you!

WHAT...
Now...
...ARE THEY TALKING ABOUT?
I DON'T KNOW ...
HE LOOKED AT US A WHILE AGO...
...SO I THINK THEY'RE TALKING ABOUT REN...

.....
EXCUSE ME, EVERYONE.
WE'RE READY...
...SO WILL YOU COME TO THE SET?
!
UH...
YES.
MS. MOMOSE, MS. OHARA.
UH.
YES, I'M COMING!
U... M...
KYOKO ...
AH.
UM...
I'LL GO GET HER–

!
End of Act 145

Skip·Beat!

Act 146: Valentine Match

SO...

YOU MADE SOMETHING ELSE FOR HIM...

...

WHAT'RE YOU GIVING HIM?

IT'S ...

IT'S NONE OF YOUR BUSI-NESS!

I don't need to tell you!

krnch
rummage
rustle
WELL...
WHAT-
EVER...

SO ANY-WAY.
rustle
rustle
POP
WHAT ...
...DO YOU THINK OF THIS?
shove
Plomp
?!
WH...
WHAT IS THIS?!
IS IT CANDY?!
With poison in it?!
No...
BUT IT'S SWEET AND IS MELTING IN MY MOUTH...
quiver
SPELLBOUND
A rich taste full of style.
This is...
CHOCOLATE!
And it must have a Royal Warrant!

SO, HOW IS IT.
Spellbound
IT'S... DELI...
tongue tied
She can't talk properly
HMM.
THEN...
...I GUESS I'LL HAVE SOME TOO.
I WAS JUST A TASTER?!
GRAB
?!
GRR
HUH?!
WHAT THE HECK?

...
ING OOOOOOOOOOOOON?!

W
...AT THE HELL IS GO
He's really confused

GRAB
SHOOOOO
Kyoko's head
...
A merciless attack and defense
Sho's head
...
Kyoko's arm

RAT A TAT TAT TAT TAT
WHAT'RE YOU DOING, YOU THOUGHTLESS IDIOT!
I'll kill you! I'll kill you three times!
BOOM
ACK ACK ACK
Oh yeah?! Kill me if you can, rah!
BOOM
BANG BANG
Image
These two are fighting for survival
!
NUHHHH
GUHHHHHHH
H...

GONNA KIIIISSSSS?!
Stop! Please stop now!
NO!
WHY'RE THEY FRENCH KISSING?!
Reality
twitch
.....

...OW LONG ARE THEY

Hawawawawawawa

flustered

Wow, amazing...

A live French kiss...

First time I've seen one.

They're staring

Even when you're acting, you don't French kiss like THAT.

TMP

SHO—VE!
!
pant pant
wheeze wheeze
...
...
WH...
WHAT ...
...WERE YOU...
... THINKING?!
...
HUH?

I DIDN'T SAY I'D GIVE IT TO YOU.
?
I ONLY LET YOU TASTE IT.
chomp
li ck
chomp
SO I TOOK IT BACK.
Hmm... mmm.
It's all right.
GRR!
HOW CHEAAAAAP!
This guy is rich! Yet he doesn't even want to give me ONE chocolate!

WELL ...
I'M DONE, SEE YA.
tmp tmp
Wait!
You thoughtless Scrooge!
TAKE!
THAT WITH YOU!
THERE'S NO REASON TO GIVE IT TO ME!
SINCE I'M NOT GOING OUT WITH THE BEAGLE!
.....
YOU HAVE ...
...A REASON NOW.
?!
WHAT'D YOU MEAN ?!
YOU'RE SO PLAIN.
YOU...

...PROBABLY HAVEN'T KISSED A GUY EVEN ONCE YET.
TO TELL THE TRUTH, I DIDN'T WANT TO DO THIS...
...BUT I DON'T WANT YOU COM-PLAINING ABOUT IT LATER...
...SO THAT'S YOURS.
IT'S MY TOKEN OF APOLOGY.

grin
twip
YOU
GO
TO

Heh...

Sff

...
Sigh
JOLT
?!
!

ka
chak

Oh.
YOU'RE BACK.
shff
kssh
HOW'S KYOKO?
slam
.....
IN A DAZE.
...
WELL ...
OF COURSE SHE IS.
That's a normal reaction.
YOU DITCHED HER, BUT NOW YOU TELL HER YOU LOVE HER.
HUH?
NO I DIDN'T.
Why would I do that? Please.
WHA ?
Oh?
sheeesh
BUT...
SHO.

YOU SAID YOU WERE GOING TO GET KYOKO BACK...
Yes.
AND YOU BOUGHT A BOUQUET THAT COST YOU SEVERAL HUNDRED THOUSAND YEN...
...AND A CHOCOLATE THAT COST 5,000 YEN...
Heh
?!
I'LL GET HER BACK.

YOU CAN'T HAVE VIE GHOUL TAKE HER AWAY.

...WAS JUST AN EXCUSE.

VIE GHOUL...

THE FLOWERS WERE JUST...

THAT'S PERFECTLY FINE FOR NOW.

IF MY PRESENCE INSIDE HER...

...IS BIGGER THAN ANYBODY ELSE'S.

VROOOOOM

VROOOOM

KYOKO...

NO.3

I WILL ...

White hair

... NOT ...

...LET YOU...
...FREE...
...EVER.

YOU...

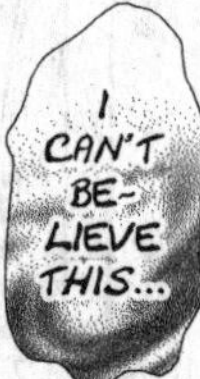
I CAN'T BE-LIEVE THIS...

...KEEP...
MY FIRST KISS... MY FIRST KISS...
STUPEFIED
...WAS STOLEN BY THAT GOOD-FOR-NOTHING...
...THINKING...

HE STOLE IT FOR SUCH A STINGY REASON...

How could he?!

WELL... I DIDN'T BELIEVE ANYMORE... THAT MY FIRST KISS WOULD BE IN A PALACE WITH A PRINCE ON A WHITE HORSE, BUT...

SOB SOB SOB

Even if you know him, it's a shock

Yes yes, I under-stand, I under-stand.

...ONLY...

A first kiss is very important for a girl.

...OF ME...

...MUCH
MORE
THAN
YESTER-
DAY...

Hmph

Wha...
LAUGH?
DID... HE JUST...
...
MR. TSURUGA?
Did he just snort?
YOUR FIRST KISS...
...
...HUH?

I DON'T GET IT...
IS IT...
...SO PRECIOUS?
Heh
IS IT SOMETHING TO CRY OVER LIKE IT'S...
...THE END OF THE WORLD?
Total Shock

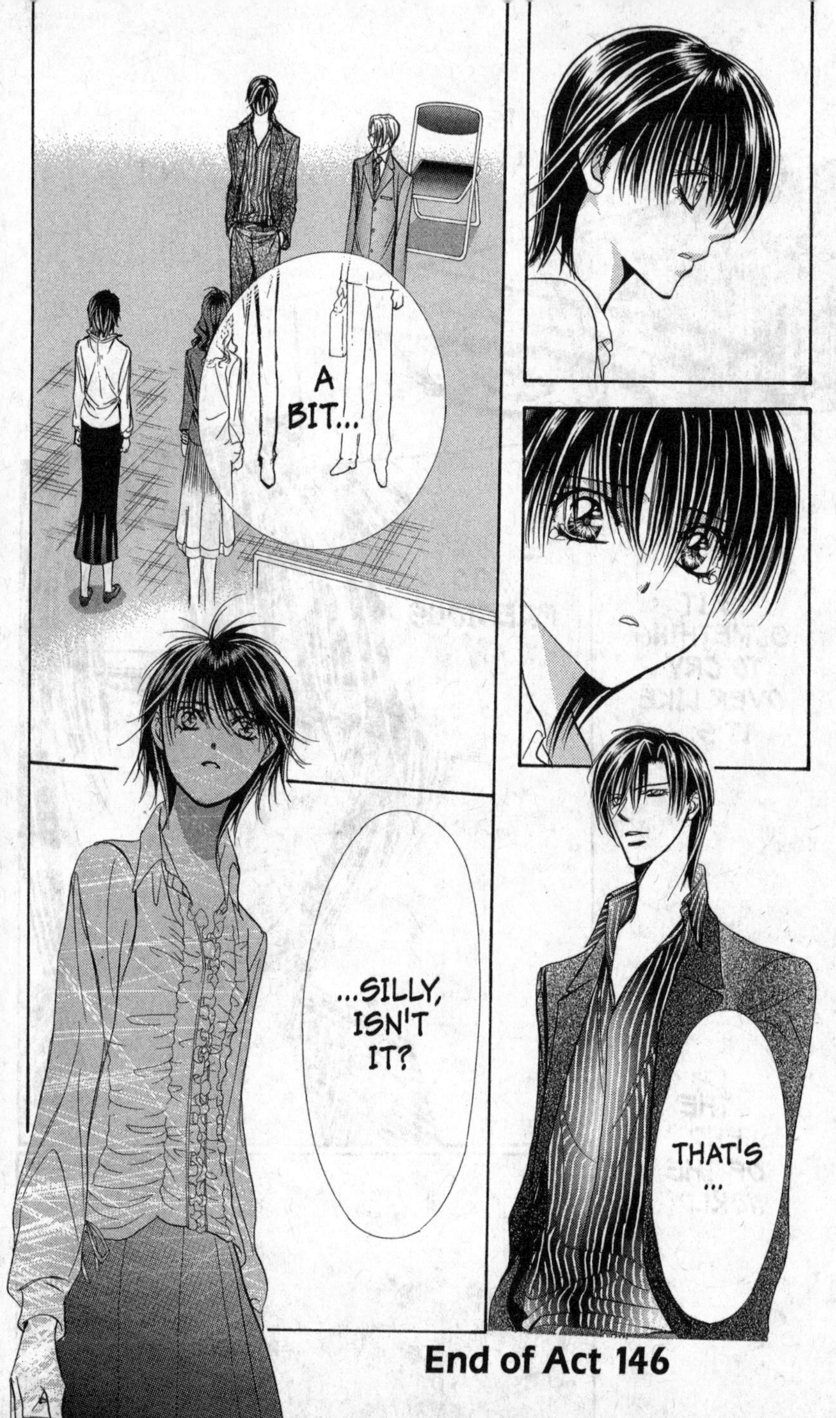
A BIT...
...SILLY, ISN'T IT?
THAT'S ...

End of Act 146

Skip·Beat!
Act 147: Valentine Weapon

THAT'S A BIT...

...SILLY, ISN'T IT?

SILLY?!
Y...
YOU SAID IT WAS SILLY?!
MR. TSURUGA?
TSURUGA? HOW COULD HE BE SO MEAN?!
...
SILLY?!
HOW COULD YOU SAY THAT?!
YOU'VE FOOLED AROUND WITH ENOUGH WOMEN SO YOUR FIRST KISS DOESN'T MEAN ANYTHING, BUT...!
KYOKO IS CRYING WITH SHOCK!
Yes.
YOU IDIOT!
THAT'S WHY I THINK IT'S SILLY.

IT'S SILLY TO CRY OVER IT.
Ah ha ha
HE SAID IT THREE TIMES!
That it's silly!
This really sucks!
HOW SILLY...
!
!
Ha

YUP...
CUZ...
...WHAT JUST HAPPENED ...
...DOESN'T COUNT AS A KISS.
IF BOTH PARTIES DON'T REALLY WANT TO KISS, IT'S NOT A KISS.
AND IF YOU COUNT A "KISS" AS WHEN YOUR LIPS TOUCH SOMEONE ELSE'S LIPS...
...MY FIRST KISS WAS BACK IN FIRST GRADE...
...WHEN I WAS RUNNING BECAUSE I WAS LATE FOR SCHOOL AND...
... SLAMMED INTO SOMEONE AS I TURNED THE CORNER.
IT WAS A PAUNCHY WORKING STIFF WITH BLUBBERY LIPS.
Unbe-lievable
A shojo manga miracle really happened!

I CAN'T REMEMBER HIS FACE ANYMORE...
...BUT I CAN STILL VIVIDLY REMEMBER...
...WHAT HE HAD FOR BREAKFAST THAT DAY.
Mr. Tsuruga...
Noooooooooo!
I wouldn't be able to bear it!
In agony
IF YOU'RE GONNA REMEMBER THE TASTE, I WANT IT TO BE CHOCOLATES, LIKE KYOKO!
That's...
...terrible...
blub blub blub
She can't help(?) crying
You can cry about it...
What a sad first kiss that was...
...for a young boy...
Pity
I WOULDN'T CRY ABOUT IT.
IT WAS AN ACCIDENT. IT DOESN'T COUNT AS A KISS.

AND I'D ALREADY SECRETLY MADE UP MY MIND...
...THAT I WANTED TO BE A PRO-FESSIONAL ACTOR...

...SO I KNEW I'D HAVE TO KISS SOMEONE FOR REAL AS PART OF MY JOB, EVEN IF I DIDN'T LIKE THE ACTRESS...
...AND I KNEW I COULDN'T BE A PRO IF IT WAS OBVIOUS I WAS ONLY ACTING, EVEN IF THE OTHER PARTY WAS ANOTHER MAN.

SO I BLUNTLY TOLD MYSELF "IF I GET HURT EACH TIME SOMETHING LIKE THIS HAPPENS...
...I'LL NEVER BE ABLE TO BECOME A PROFESSIONAL ACTOR."

MR. TSURUGA WAS THINKING LIKE THAT AS A CHILD...
...
OF COURSE THERE'S NO WAY WE CAN COMPETE AGAINST SOMEONE LIKE HIM ...

I SEE...

BUT I'M AIMING TO BECOME AN ACTRESS...

...SO I MAY HAVE TO ACT OUT A KISSING SCENE SOMEDAY...

HE'S RIGHT... I'VE NEVER THOUGHT ABOUT IT BEFORE...

I MAY HAVE TO KISS SOME-ONE I HARDLY KNOW...

And maybe I'll even have to kiss an actress...

IF I WANT TO BECOME A FIRST-CLASS ACTRESS...

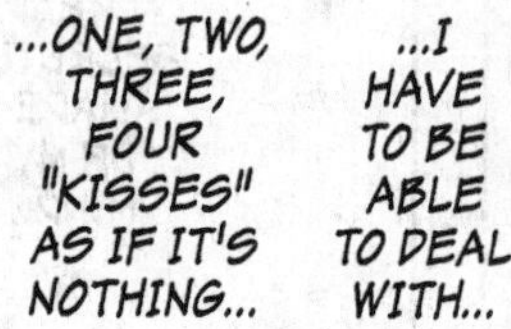

...I HAVE TO BE ABLE TO DEAL WITH...
...ONE, TWO, THREE, FOUR "KISSES" AS IF IT'S NOTHING...

THE DETAILS OF YOUR FIRST KISS...
...DEPEND ON HOW YOU INTERPRET IT.

WHAT YOU FEEL IS YOUR FIRST KISS...
...COUNTS AS YOUR REAL FIRST KISS.
IT MIGHT SOUND PUSHY...
...BUT DEALING WITH IT THAT WAY...
...IS...
...WHAT WE ACTORS HAVE TO LEARN TO DO.
IT'S THE RULE OF THE HEART.
I HOPE...
...YOU'LL BE ABLE TO PRACTICE IT SOON.

UH...
YES!
IT LOOKS AS IF REN'S GIVING FRIENDLY ADVICE AS HER COLLEAGUE ...
I JUST HAPPENED TO FEED AN ANTEATER WITH MY MOUTH!
And his tongue just happened to get inside my mouth!
YES YES, YOU'RE DOING IT WELL.
...BUT HE'S JUST TRYING TO MAKE KYOKO FORGET ABOUT THAT KISS...
Sho...
...Is being called an ant-eater.

TOUCHING LIPS WITH A BEAST DOES NOT COUNT AS A KISS AT ALL!

Therefore I am still a pure virgin! The sacred girl Kyoko! The holy girl Kyoko!

Yes yes.

YOU'RE RIGHT.

AND HE SUCCEEDED.

AH.

BUT MS. MOGAMI.

YES?

THIS "RULE OF THE HEART FOR ACTORS"...

IT ALWAYS WORKS WHEN YOU'RE ACTING...

...BUT IN PRIVATE, YOU CAN'T USE IT AGAINST THE SAME PERSON TWICE.

Wha?

REALLY?!

OF COURSE NOT...

Oh!

So it only works while you're acting!

YES.

BUT YOU'RE RIGHT. IT'S THE RULE OF THE HEART OF ACTORS.

tmp

SO.

WATCH YOURSELF FROM NOW ON.

THERE'S ...
...NO SECOND CHANCE.

!

THIS GUY!

HE LET HIS TRUE FEELINGS SLIP!

That he'll never forgive her if Fuwa manages to kiss her again!

smile

O-Of course I shall risk my life to preserve my purity!

GOOD.

Well...

I GUESS THINGS LIKE THIS WON'T HAPPEN VERY OFTEN.

BUT YOU SHOULD STILL WATCH OUT ANYWAY.
Yes!
I shall take your warning to heart!
GOOD.
.....
REN...
HE...
...PUT HIS TRUE FEELINGS INTO WORDS FOR THE FIRST TIME...
...WHEN HE USED TO BURY THEM DEEP IN HIS HEART.

...MUST
BE...
...REALLY
REALLY
PISSED
ABOUT
IT...

End of Act 147

Skip·Beat!

Act 148: Valentine's Day XXXX

HE SEEMS TO BE IN A PRETTY GOOD MOOD NOW.
I wonder about that expression... but it's better than the Nio statue at least.
YES...HE'S MANAGING SOMEHOW.
Thank you.
grin grin grin

SOMETHING GOOD HAPPENED ...
...WHEN HE WENT TO SEE KYOKO.
Maybe they're going out again?
I WONDER ...
I DON'T KNOW THE DETAILS.
Because I didn't go inside with him.
OH.
REALLY?
BUT ...

HE...
...MUST HAVE...

For sure.

HE'S SMILING...
...SO FEARLESSLY AND CONFIDENTLY...

YES.

HE EASILY WON AGAINST THE VIE GHOUL VOCALIST.

And moreover.

HE MUST'VE DONE SOMETHING...

...TO EVEN WIN AGAINST...

...REN TSURUGA...

GEEZ... WHAT DID HE DO?

Really...

I SHOULDN'T HAVE LET HIM GO INSIDE ALONE.

tmp
slide
SHE'S SO EASY...
...TO FIGURE OUT.

SHE MUST'VE BEEN THINK-ING...
You know!
Adorable
Your first kiss is with your prince to seal your love forever, and I'll be wearing a dress like a princess at a church that looks like a castle!
DREAM
Kyaaaaaah!
BUT NOW HER FIRST KISS WAS STOLEN BY ME, WHO SHE HATES, FOR A RIDICULOUS REASON...
...SO SHE MUST BE THINKING ...
Hmph
... SOMETHING LIKE THAT.
Initial shock
When she snaps out of it...
Her anger starts to simmer at the new reality.
...
...

AND NOW...
SHOOOTAROOO!
I will not forgive yooou!
HOW DARE YOU STEAL MY LIPS WHEN I HAVEN'T EVEN GOTTEN MARRIED YET!
This grudge! I'll chase you to the end of hell to get you~~!
BOOOOM
SHE MUST BE LIKE THAT...
...ALL SHE CAN THINK OF IS ME!
grin
CHASE ME. TO WHEREVER.

BE LIKE YOU USED TO BE, WHEN ALL YOU THOUGHT ABOUT WAS ME.

GET ANGRIER.

AND...

DRIVE EVERYTHING OUT OF YOUR MIND EXCEPT ME.

...YOU'RE GONNA BE OBSESSED WITH ME...

...MORE THAN YOU USED TO BE...

HATE, HATE ME...
...EVEN MORE AND MORE!
Heh heh heh
A warped sense of possess-iveness
NOW, KYOKO!

THINK ABOUT ME!
You know!
Adorable
Your first kiss is with your prince to seal your love forever, and I'll be wearing a dress like a princess at a church that looks like a castle!
ROMANTIC DREAM
Kyaaaaaah!
Of course, of course my prince...
...is Sho!
OOOOOOOOH
Hey Kyoko, you fool! How could you?!

Oh!

!

OH NO!

Now I remember.

I WAS LOOKING FOR MY LUNCH BOX...

A classmate who's a Sho fan threw Kyoko's lunch box away.

...SO I SHOULDN'T BE IMAGINING THINGS WITH A RESORT FLYER I FOUND IN THE GARBAGE!

But she keeps it.

From the flyer

I GOTTA HURRY. LUNCHTIME WILL BE OVER SOON.

rummage

I CAN FORGET ABOUT THE LUNCH BOX, BUT I WANT TO FIND THE CHOPSTICKS AT LEAST.

rummage

THEY'RE PRECIOUS CHOPSTICKS THE OKAMISAN* BOUGHT FOR ME.

*Sho's mom

Ah!

Blah
Blah
Blah
Blah

BACK THEN ...
...I NEVER THOUGHT ...
No, THAT does NOT COUNT as a kiss!
...HE'D STEAL MY FIRST KISS...
Blah
Blah
Blah
Blah
...AND MAKE ME...
I REMEMBERED ...
... SOMETHING I DIDN'T WANT TO...
Because she saw the rolling chopstick
NOW I...
Your first kiss is with your prince to seal your love forever, and I'll be wearing a dress like a princess at a church that looks like a castle!
... REMEMBER THE FOOLISH THINGS I THOUGHT...
Of course of course, my prince ...
...is Sho!
...UNTIL LAST YEAR.
...SO FURIOUS ...
EVEN THOUGH I'VE MADE UP MY MIND TO NEVER FALL IN LOVE AGAIN...
EVEN THOUGH I WASN'T PLANNING ON SAVING MY FIRST KISS FOR SOMEONE.
Actually, I'd forgotten about my first kiss fantasy completely.

STILL...
WHEN I THINK ABOUT HOW MY FIRST KISS...
...WAS STOLEN FOR SUCH A STUPID REASON...
...MY BLOOD BOILS, EVEN THOUGH I'VE RECOVERED FROM THE SHOCK!
GNNN
NNNNNNNH
GAH...
SHOTAROOOO! HOW DARE YOU STEAL THE LIPS OF A PURE MAIDEN FOR SUCH A REASON!

I WILL NOT FORGIVE YOOOOOOOU!
BOOM!
MAGMAAAAAA
THIS GRUDGE! I WILL STALK YOU UNTIL YOU'RE BORN AGAIN TO HAVE MY REVENGE!
She's fallen in his trap.
.....
KYO...
...KO?

Oh!

!

YOU ALL RIGHT?

...

UH...

Yes! It's fine!

Look!

It's still clean, and there's no dirt on it!

If I Believed in the 15-second rule, I could use it just fine!

NO... I DIDN'T ASK ABOUT THE CHOP-STICK...

...

BUT I DON'T THINK IT'S VERY HYGIENIC, SO I'LL GO GET A NEW PAIR.

TODAY THERE'RE LOTS OF CHOCOLATE DESSERTS.
Cuz it's Valentine's.
Look, look.
I GOT ONE OF EACH.
Are you stupid ?!

You'll gain weight again! For sure!
I don't care! ♡
Chomp
Mmm.

It's melting in my mouth and it's so delicious! ♡
CRACKLE
MELTING
BUT IT'S SWEET AND IS MELTING IN MY MOUTH...
No...
SPELLBOUND
I WAS JUST A TASTER!!
shiver
shake
K...
KYOOOOKOOOO.
Hey, pull yourself together.
E... EXCUSE ME.
I'LL GO GET THE CHOPSTICKS.
Please start eating.
...
KYOKO...
...STILL HASN'T GOTTEN OVER IT.
She keeps looking scary.
Oh!
EVEN IF SHE TELLS HERSELF THAT WASN'T A KISS...

...FUWA KISSED HER...
...SO...
...IT MIGHT BE DIFFICULT TO FORGET ABOUT IT...

TOSS

Sigh

AH, THIS SUCKS...

WHATEVER I SEE OR HEAR REMINDS ME OF SHOTARO AND I GET ANGRY!

Falling into his trap even more

Dish Return

I can't stand the smell of chocolate either... I remember everything so vividly I get pissed.

AH... DARN... IF I KEEP ON LIKE THIS, I'LL REMEMBER WHAT HAPPENED WITH HIM EVERY YEAR AROUND VALENTINE'S...

...AND FEEL IRRITATED AND ANGRY THE WHOLE DAY AND HAVE MY HEART AND BODY EATEN AWAY...

sway sway

GRR GRR

GRR GRR

No. Valentine chocolates go on sale in January.

Ugh...

I'D GOTTEN TO THE POINT WHERE I MANAGED NOT TO THINK OF HIM DAY AND NIGHT...

...BUT NOW I'M BACK TO THE WAY I USED TO BE...

NO.

rustle

VALENTINE'S IS NOW A NIGHTMARE FESTIVAL INSTEAD OF VAIN DAY.

IT'S EVEN WORSE NOW.

...
RIGHT SIZE.
peek

MR. TSURUGA.
HMM?
UM...
WHAT IS IT?
Heh
YOU'RE BEING SO FORMAL.
EXCUSE ME... DO YOU HAVE SOME TIME AFTER THIS?
?
YES I DO...
...
UUUUUM...
There's...

THERE'S...
Uh...
...SOMETHING...
...I'D...
...LIKE...
...TO...
...GIVE...
...TO YOU...
MR. REN TSURUGA

...
...
MS. MOGAMI?
...
UM...
I THOUGHT IT MIGHT BE GOOD FOR AN AFTER-LUNCH TREAT...
...SO...
...I MADE...
...THIS WINE GELEE...

I THOUGHT...
...IF I GAVE YOU CHOCOLATES TOO...
...IT'D BE ANNOYING FOR YOU...
...SO...
...I WAS THINKING...
...THAT I'D GIVE YOU...
...SOMETHING THAT'D BE EASY TO EAT...
...FOR VALENTINE'S.
AND SOMETHING...
..."EASY TO EAT" TURNED OUT TO BE...
...A SIMPLE GELATIN...
...
AH...
SO ONLY I...

Thank you
Hee
...GOT SOMETHING OTHER THAN CHOCOLATES...
MAY I EAT IT?
!
Yes...
...
Rose-colored
DEJA VU?
Am I just imagining it? I think I've seen this before...
He's not interested in sweets, so he only glanced at the spoons.
...
THE SPOON I BROUGHT FROM HOME WAS A LITTLE SHORT COMPARED TO THE GLASS...
She realized it this morning in her rehearsal room.
I was such a fool...
I WAS ONLY THINKING OF THE GLASS WHEN I MADE THE GELEE.
Yes.
...SO I BORROWED THE SPOON FROM THE CAFETERIA, BECAUSE IT WAS JUST THE RIGHT LENGTH.
OH...

I CAN SEE WHY.
I CAN SEE THE RED OF THE GELEE THROUGH THE CRYSTAL ROSES...
...AND IT'S BEAUTIFUL.
Isn't it?!
When I first saw this glass, I could imagine the gelee in it and I writhed with joy!
shiver
YES... YOU WOULD LOVE THIS SORT OF GLASS.
Because... because this glass...
...looks like Queen Rosa, doesn't it?!
So I thought I had to get this if I was going to give you wine gelee!
IT'S...

... DANGER-OUS...
...TO THINK...
...THAT MAYBE SHE'S TREATING ME...
...SPECIALLY...
yeah.
I'M SO GLAD ...
THIS IS THE FIRST TIME I MADE WINE GELEE...
...SO I WAS WORRIED ABOUT WHAT WOULD HAPPEN...
Calm
I CAN'T STOP EATING. THIS IS DELICIOUS.
REALLY ?!
He's learned his lesson many times
...IF YOU DIDN'T LIKE IT...

NO NO...
YOU CAN'T FOOL ME WITH THAT EXPRESSION.
Not at all.
I'm all right.
I...
...WILL NOT BE SWAYED ...

?!
Dilated pupils
Her veins are show-ing
A big frown
Her brain has been completely contam-inated by Fuwa Syndrome
Hannya
.....
tink

SO I WAS WORRIED ABOUT WHAT WOULD HAPPEN...
...IF YOU DIDN'T LIKE IT...

I THOUGHT WHAT I FIND DELICIOUS MIGHT BE TOO CHILDISH FOR YOU...
...SO UNTIL I GOT IT RIGHT...

Hannya
And so...
GRR GRR
GRR GRR
GRRRR
SIMMER
...
...
...
creak

MS. MOGAMI.

End of Act 148

Skip·Beat!
Act 149: A Poisoned Flower

IT'S LIKE...

...I'VE RETURNED...

WHEN WHAT-EVER I SAW...
...IN THOSE DAYS...
...HE WAS ALREADY SHORT TEMPERED, SELF-CENTERED, FULL OF HIM-SELF, AND A SHOW-OFF!
YES!
I REMEMBER NOW! WE WERE JUST PLAYING, BUT HE ALWAYS BLAMED ME WHEN HE MADE MISTAKES!
SHOOM
Even something ordinary like
...AND HEARD...
They said they couldn't ...
...stay with me, that I'm too selfish.
TOOM
Selfish
Self-centered
Overconfident
Top 3 Pronouns to Describe Shotaro Fuwa
...how much...
...FILLED MY HEAD WITH HIM.
...you loved me.
SHO!
...I WOULD BE ENJOYING MY SECOND YEAR OF HIGH SCHOOL!
KSSS!
SHOTAROO!!
WHEN I THINK THAT YOU'RE IN YOUR SECOND YEAR OF HIGH SCHOOL, I GO CRAZY WITH A GRUDGE!
EVILAURA
slither
slither
slither

MY SENSES...

...ARE TRAPPED BY HIM.

AND I CAN'T DO...
...ANY-THING TO FREE MYSELF...

...FROM THE POISON ...
creak
MS. MOGAMI.
...THAT HAS...
...IN-VADED MY BODY.

creak
WHA...
WHA
...?

Kiss

THE WINE GELEE WAS REALLY...

...DELICIOUS.

BOOM
WHOOOOOOOOSH
Whaaa?!
Waaaaaaaah
Aaaah~~
All the Shotaro that was in her brain.

WHAAAAAT?!

Thank you.
I'm...
...so happy!
TOSS
Hey ...
Uh...
Hey, Hio!
What're you doing?!
YOU CAN HAVE THOSE TOO.
YOU CAN EAT OR DRINK THEM, WHAT-EVER.
tmp tmp
Panic panic
SHEESH.
WHY'RE YOU SO ANGRY?!
YOU ACT SO DIFFERENT IN PUBLIC AND PRIVATE.
I'M JUST BEING CONSIDERATE. I'M REACTING THE WAY PEOPLE WANT ME TO.
So you're being a hypocrite.
MOST BOYS WOULD BE HAPPY IF THEY GOT CHOCOLATES ON VALENTINE'S.
Hmph.
SO WHY WOULD I BE HAPPY?

EVEN YOU MUST UNDERSTAND WHAT THOSE WOMEN WERE THINKING...
...WHEN THEY GAVE ME THOSE CHOCO-LATES.
HUH?
What?
Hio is sOOOO Cuuuuute.
He's so tiny! ♡
Tee ♥ hee! ♥
He'll be a seventh-grader this year, but he's just too cuuuute.
He's so tiny! ♡
That's all I can think of.
Hmm~
SO THEY DIDN'T TREAT YOU LIKE A "GUY"...
mumble mumble
MATSUDA...
How dare you...
WHEN YOU'RE TALKING TO YOURSELF, DO IT SILENTLY.

The ban-hammer for Ms. Matsuda

Waah

She often makes comments that make him angry.

I'M NOT STUPID ENOUGH TO BE HAPPY ABOUT GETTING CHOCOLATES THAT...

...DON'T EVEN COUNT AS OBLIG-ATORY ONES.

I'm not a kid who gets happy from simply getting a lot of chocolate.

Well, happy happy.

Kanaaaeeeaaaeee!♡ Our happy day has finally arrived!

tmp tmp

OOPS...

I'm ready to accept them anytime...

Your chocolates and your confession of love!

Now now, come come.

HE IS ANNOYING AS USUAL.

I'LL GO TO HIO'S REHEARSAL ROOM QUICK AND SHOO HIM AWAY.

Hey

Kanae, there's no need to be shy.

Don't make me wait.

IGNORE

This must be my chocolates! ♡
UH.
grab
HEY!
GIVE IT BACK! THEY'RE NOT FOR YOU!
What?!
COME ON, YOU DON'T NEED TO WAIT FOR THE PERFECT TIME TO GIVE THEM TO ME. ♡
You're so cute!
KANAE, YOU JUST NEED TO SHOVE THEM AT ME AND I'LL ACCEPT THEM.
Ah ha ha ha ha
.....
ARGH!
I'M TELLING YOU THEY'RE NOT FOR YOU!
How could you be so stupid?!
MO!
DON'T PLAY AROUND WITH THAT. GIVE IT BACK NOW!
NO.
Ha ha ha
You're so cute for getting angry.
I TOLD YOU IT'S ALL RIGHT. JUST GIVE THEM TO ME.

HEY YOU.
UH.
Tch
YOU'RE HARASSING THE WOMAN YOU LIKE AND HAVING FUN AT HER EXPENSE. ARE YOU TWELVE?
Wha?
A KID CALLED ME A KID!
SHE WANTS IT BACK...
...SO GIVE IT BACK.
YOU'RE OVER 20, RIGHT? YOU'RE A GROWNUP, YET YOU'RE ACTING LIKE A CHILD.
It's so embarrassing, I couldn't bear to watch.
...
I mean...
WHEN I THINK ABOUT STUPID GUYS LIKE YOU RUNNING SOCIETY...

...IT CRUSHES MY HEART WITH FEAR.
What's gonna happen to my future?
Heh
A faraway look
......
PFFT.

.....

DON'T GET SO COCKY ...
...YOU BRAT.
YOU ...
...THINK I'M AVOIDING YOU CUZ I HATE KIDS.

ARE YOU STUPID?
Of course that's not why.
I'M AVOIDING YOU CUZ I'M...

... SCARED OF YOU!
YOU'RE THE FOOL!
How could you say it out loud?! That's not something you should just admit like that!
...

I DON'T WANT TO BE HONEST WITH YOU...
...AND HAVE YOUR PARENTS HATE ME.

I...

...HATE...
...HAVING TO MOVE MY BODY TO MEET A CHILD'S EYES...
...AND HAVING TO MOVE MY MOUTH SO I SPEAK LIKE A CHILD.
I HATE KIDS...
...SO THERE'S NO WAY I CAN HIDE MY DISLIKE FOR YOU...
...EVEN IF YOUR FAMILY IS ALL IN SHOWBIZ.
BUT YOU WOULDN'T LIKE ME ACTING THAT WAY.
IF YOU SNITCH TO YOUR PARENTS AND GET ME ON THE WRONG SIDE OF THE BIGWIGS...
...I'LL HAVE TROUBLE SURVIVING IN SHOWBIZ.

THAT'S WHY I TOOK THE TROUBLE OF AVOIDING YOU.
...
WHAT THE HELL...?
I THOUGHT HE WAS JUST STUPID...
...BUT HE'S AN EVEN WORSE SORT OF IDIOT.
A simple fool would've Been Better...
IN ANY CASE ...

...IT'S NOT A REASON YOU CAN BE PROUD OF.
HEY, YOU BRAT.
DON'T GET THINGS WRONG.
PEOPLE IN THIS BUSINESS TREAT YOU WELL BECAUSE THEY'RE AFRAID OF YOUR FAMILY...
...AND NOT BECAUSE THEY RESPECT YOU.

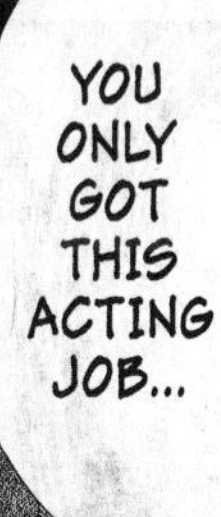
YOU ONLY GOT THIS ACTING JOB...

...BECAUSE YOUR PARENTS ARE BIG-NAME ACTORS.
!

OH? WHAT'S WITH YOUR FACE?
MAYBE YOU JUST NOW REALIZED IT?
...
YOU'RE SO STUPID.
THIS IS WHY I HATE KIDS. THEY'RE SO SIMPLE.
SECOND AND THIRD GENERATION TALENTO ALWAYS HAVE A CLEAR PATH EVEN IF THEY'VE GOT NO TALENT.
YOU'RE ONLY WALKING ON THE ROAD YOUR PARENTS PAVED FOR YOU.
...
HOW COULD YOU ...?

YOU CAN SURVIVE IN SHOWBIZ...
...BUT NOT BECAUSE YOU'VE GOT TALENT.
YOU'RE JUST TAKING ADVAN-TAGE...
...OF YOUR FAMOUS PAR-ENTS' ...
... NAME-
GRAB
HIO...
REMEMBER THIS, ALL RIGHT?

KA
DO—OM

EX-CUSE ME...
SHE KEEPS FREEZ-ING...
SHE WAS ACTING FINE BEFORE LUNCH.
HMM...
SHE FREEZES IN DIFFERENT PLACES, SO IT'S NOT AS IF SHE'S FORGOTTEN HER LINES.
...
I WONDER WHAT HAPPENED TO KYOKO...

.....

Hmm...

tmp

THEN...

WILL YOU CONCENTRATE ON YOUR ROLE DURING YOUR BREAK?

Yes, I will for sure!

ALL RIGHT.

WE'LL SHOOT SOME OTHER SCENES FIRST.

I'M REALLY SORRY...

DON'T WORRY.

EVEN ATHLETES HAVE A HARD TIME CONCEN-TRATING ONCE THEY'VE LOST THEIR STRIDE.

BUT...

...KYOKO.

YES...

IF YOU CAN'T SOLVE THIS PROBLEM ON YOUR OWN...

...COME TO ME FOR HELP...

EVEN...

...IF I CAN'T SOLVE THIS PROBLEM...

SORRY EVERYONE. WE'LL SHOOT SCENE 70 FIRST.
Uh
YEEES.
rattle rattle
We'll clear the set then.
Blah Blah

WHAT-EVER...

Blah Blah

...I CAN'T TELL YOU ABOUT IT...

WHAT SHOULD I DO?

...DI-RECTOR OGATA... I...

THIS IS BEAU-TIFUL.

THIS IS DELI-CIOUS.

MIO.

THANK YOU...!

THANK YOU...

...I...
...SEE...
...OR HEAR...
...MAKES MY HEAD...
...FULL OF THAT MAN.
MY SENSES...
...ARE TRAPPED BY HIM.

AND I...

...CAN'T DO ANYTHING TO FREE MYSELF.

...IS INVADING ...

...MY...

...EVERY-THING...

THAT MAN...

End of Act 149

Skip·Beat!
Act 150: A Faint Scar

I'LL CALL YOU SHOTA!

GO AHEAD!

I MUCH PREFER THAT TO BEING CALLED "KANAAAAAE" BY YOU.

LET'S GO, HIO.
tmp
tmp
...
...
I'll tell everyone you're a shota actress!
I'm serious!
In tears

...
KANAE ...
Hey...
PEOPLE... REALLY WILL CALL YOU A SHOTA ACTRESS ...
He WILL tell every-one about it.
CUZ YOU ...
tmp tmp
tmp

...GAVE ME THIS...
In the bag are...
Kanae's choco-lates

PLEASE ACCEPT THIS...
...HIO.

Isn't that amazing?
THIS IS THE FIRST TIME I'VE GIVEN SOMEONE CHOCO-LATES ON VALEN-TINE'S.
Isn't that precious?
THIS IS THE FIRST TIME EVER THAT I MADE HAND-MADE CHOCO-LATES.

THIS IS THE FIRST AND LAST TIME I'LL EVER DO SOME-THING LIKE THIS.
Isn't this a miracle ?

I REALLY WANT YOU TO ACCEPT THIS ASSORTMENT OF MY FIRST EXPERIENCES!

Oh no, I said it, I'm so embarrassed, kyaaaah!

UH... I'M NOT TOO HAPPY ABOUT THIS...
Getting chocolates this way...
Kanae, you look scary.
.....
.....

SHE'S COMPLETELY TAKING ADVANTAGE OF ME...
...TO BREAK HIS HEART.

And HIS heart was broken as well
WELL, ALL RIGHT... I DID VOLUNTEER TO KEEP HIM AWAY.
SORRY FOR FORCING THOSE CHOCO-LATES ON YOU, HIO.

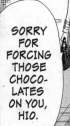

BUT IT'S TRUE I MADE THEM MYSELF BECAUSE I WANTED TO GIVE THEM TO YOU.
I wanted to thank you for keeping that idiot away.
I...
IT'S... ALL RIGHT...
shlup

I DON'T MIND, BUT YOU MIGHT REALLY END UP AS A SHOTA ACTRESS.
The choco-lates were bad enough...
BUT YOU DE-FENDED ME AS WELL...

... LIKE THAT.

STOMP

Right after she threw the idiot down.

DO YOU THINK ACTING IS SUCH AN EASY JOB?!

ACTING FAILS WHEN THE VIEWER IS TURNED OFF BY IT!

YOU DON'T KEEP GETTING JOBS JUST BECAUSE YOU'RE A THOROUGH-BRED!

YOU DON'T TAKE ACTING SERI-OUSLY AT ALL.
EVEN IF THE PUBLIC ALLOWS YOU TO ACT SUPERIOR TOWARDS HIO, I WON'T!

HIO IS ONE OF THE FEW REAL ACTORS THAT I...
...TRULY RE-SPECT!
YEAH... AND YOU SAID...
Respect... Anyone would think you're nuts...
BUT...
...IT'S TRUE.
THE FIRST TIME I WORKED WITH YOU...
...I FELT...
...LIKE I LOST.

...WAS CONFIDENT THAT I COULD CRY BETTER THAN ANYBODY.

UNTIL ...

...YOUR "MAKOTO," WHOSE PARENTS DIED IN FRONT OF HIS EYES...

... BECAME A LIFE-LESS SHELL ...

...AND CRIED SILENTLY...

...WITH-OUT RAISING HIS VOICE OR BLINK-ING...

...EVERYONE CAN TELL YOU'RE CRYING.

MY ACTING ONLY APPEALED TO PEOPLE'S EYES.

IT DIDN'T AFFECT THE VIEWER'S HEARTS AT ALL.

THAT SORT OF POWER DIDN'T FLOW OUT...

...WITH MY TEARS...
...
WELL ...

I DON'T THINK ABOUT WHAT THE VIEWERS WILL THINK WHEN I ACT.

I JUST GOT REAL SAD WHEN I REMEMBERED THE TIME MY GRANDMA DIED...

That means...

I JUST HAPPENED TO BE IN SYNC WITH WHAT MY ROLE WAS FEELING.

Heh heh

YOUR ACTING IS REAL BECAUSE YOU CAN ACT BEFORE YOU THINK.

tmp

I...

...WOULDN'T HAVE ADMITTED HOW IMMATURE MY ACTING WAS...

tmp

tmp

...IF IT WASN'T YOU WHO MADE ME REALIZE IT.

I'd have turned a blind eye after being shocked and angry.

tmp
SO...
tmp
tmp
THANK YOU...
...FOR GIVING ME...
...A CHANCE TO GROW.

FROM NOW ON...
...I'LL DO MY BEST SO I DON'T END UP AS AN ACTRESS WHO'S SIMPLY SATISFIED...
...IF SHE'S "ACTING."
I'LL...
...GET GOOD ...
...SO THAT NO ONE CAN SAY IT'S "BECAUSE YOU COME FROM A FAMILY OF ACTORS."

LET'S DO OUR BEST.
YEAH.

WHAP

KYOKO STARTED ACTING STRANGE AFTER SHE WAS ALONE WITH YOU AFTER LUNCH.
THAT MEANS YOU MUST'VE DONE SOME-THING!
I can imagine what you did to her!
How could you be so lecherous!
And at work!
You suck!
You're a grownup, so restrain yourself!
I GUESS MR. YASHIRO IS IMAGINING SOMETHING VERY EXTREME...
I wouldn't do anything like that at work.
BUT ...
Ha ha
YOU'RE RIGHT.
I HAVEN'T DONE ANYTHING THAT WOULD MAKE YOU WRITHE WITH ANGER...
...BUT SHE'S PROBABLY FREEZING UP BECAUSE OF ME...
...
...SO I'LL DO SOMETHING ABOUT IT.

HAVEN'T DONE ANYTHING THAT WOULD MAKE ME WRITHE WITH ANGER?

THAT MEANS...

!

HE WAS STILL LECHEROUS!

How could you do something so obscene at work! I won't condone it!

What did he first think Ren did to Kyoko?

HMM...

I STOPPED MYSELF AT THE LAST MOMENT POSSIBLE...

I...

...WAS GONNA DO THE SAME THING...

...THAT FUWA DID WITHOUT HESI-TATING...

WHEN I SAW...
...THAT SHE...
MELTING
CRACKLE
It's melting in my mouth and it's so delicious! ♡
shiver
shake
Hannya
And so...
...WAS STILL TRAPPED BY FUWA...
...I WANTED TO REPLACE THAT...
...MEMORY...
...SO SHE WOULD ALWAYS REMEMBER ME...
...EVERY TIME SHE THOUGHT ABOUT HER KISS WITH FUWA.
SO SHE'D REMEMBER...
...MY KISS...
BUT...
...I DIDN'T...

EVEN IF...
...IT WAS A ONCE IN A LIFE-TIME OPPOR-TUNITY...
...I DIDN'T WANT THOSE...
...DARK MURKY FEELINGS...
...TO BE A PART OF THE MOMENT...
...I WAS ALLOWED...
...TO TOUCH HER.
MORE-OVER...
...I DIDN'T WANT TO CONFUSE HER...
...WITH AN ACT OF EGO.

WELL ...
....SHE'S ALREADY CONFUSED COM-PLETELY.
Just as I'd planned.
twirl twirl
twirl twirl
whirl-pool
whirl-pool
gasp gasp
gasp gasp
A whirlpool of Tsuruga
She's fallen into his trap
AND I ONLY KISSED HER CHEEK ...
I WONDER WHAT WOULD'VE HAPPENED IF I'D DONE WHAT I'D FIRST PLANNED...
She might've thrown herself off a building in shock...
Kyoko
RE-FRESH... RE-FRESH YOUR MIND.
twirl twirl
Don't think too hard
DON'T THINK ABOUT ANY-THING.
sway sway
I'M GLAD I STOPPED MYSELF ...
AH... NO NO...
HURRY... I'VE GOT TO CON-CENTRATE ON MY ROLE QUICK...
SMACK
Concentrate.

AAAAAAAAAAA AAAAAAAAA~~H!
.....
whirl-pool
twirl twirl
gasp gasp
gasp gasp
whirl-pool
twirl twirl
MY...
... OBJECTIVE WAS TO FILL HER HEAD WITH ME, SO SHE COULDN'T THINK OF FUWA ANYMORE...
BUT...
...
... SHE'LL BE HURT IF SHE HAS ...
NO... I CAN'T ...
twirl twirl
I CAN'T BECOME MIO...
...DOING HER JOB PROPERLY ...
... PROB-LEMS ...
sob... sob...
sob
I'M NO GOOD AFTER ALL...
shp

MS. MOGAMI?
BA
DUMP
gawp
BWAAAA!
The reaction he dreamed of.
...
Ha
Uh... no no
MS. MOGAMI.
ARE YOU...
...THINKING ABOUT WHAT I DID TO YOU?
JOLT
!
UH... REALLY?

Come on.
WHY'D YOU TAKE IT SO SERIOUSLY?
mumble
I can't under-stand...
IT WAS JUST A THANK-YOU KISS.
IF YOU OVER-REACT EVERY TIME I KISS YOUR CHEEK...
...I WON'T EVER BE ABLE TO THANK YOU.
SHEESH... YOU'RE SO DISTURBED YOU CAN'T EVEN DO YOUR JOB PROPERLY.
mumble
YOU'RE AN ENDANGERED SPECIES... YOU SHOULD HAVE THE STATE PROTECT YOU.
mumble
...
I CAN HEAR YOU... MR. TSURUGA...
Oh?
UH, YOU CAN?
SORRY, SORRY. I DIDN'T MEAN TO ACCUSE YOU.
HOW-EVER.
YOU'RE INCONVEN-IENCING EVERYONE, WASTING THEIR TIME OVER SOMETHING TRIVIAL LIKE A THANK-YOU KISS.
STAB
Inconvien-iencing
SO GET YOUR ACT TOGETHER, SINCE YOU'RE A PROFES-SIONAL.
STAB
A professional
Inconvien-iencing
That's what I wanted to say.

SO...
...YOU'RE NOT... ACCUSING ME?
GLARE
HUH?
You are seriously...
...accusing me...
Oh.
THAT'S HOW YOU TOOK IT?
Yes!
YOU MADE IT SEEM AS IF IT WAS JUST MY FAULT...
IF YOU HADN'T DONE WHAT YOU DID...
...I... I...
Wouldn't be going around in circles in a whirlpool...
Uh, all right.
YES, YES.
I'M TO BLAME EVEN IF I DIDN'T MEAN TO, RIGHT?
I under-stand.

SORRY, SORRY.
I'm sorry. Dui Bu Qi. Lo siento mucho.
HE DOESN'T SEEM SINCERE AT ALL...
Unre-pentant
GRR
FOR A MOMENT... I SAW...
...MR. TSURUGA'S HIDDEN SIDE.
WHAT DO YOU MEAN?
My hidden side?
A LADIES' MAN.
HE DOESN'T JUST PRETEND TO BE A GENTLE-MAN...
...
WHY WOULD YOU THINK THAT?
YOU ALWAYS CASUALLY KISS WOMEN HERE AND THERE, SO YOU END UP DOING IT WITHOUT THINKING.
HOW CAN YOU SAY THAT? I DON'T ALWAYS DO IT.
I ONLY DO IT OCCA-SION-ALLY.
A distinc-tion
SO YOU DO!
WHEN I...
...WORK WITH FOREIGN MODELS, YES.

I DON'T DENY EXPRESSING HAPPINESS AND JOY WHEN I'M WITH THEM.

Hugs and kisses on the cheek.

I see...

YES ...

MR. TSURUGA MUST HAVE FREQUENT CONTACT WITH FOREIGNERS ...

SO IF YOU ASK ME WHETHER I END UP ACTING THE SAME WAY IN MY EVERYDAY LIFE...

...THIS IS WHAT I DO.

SO YOU MAY BE RIGHT.

I MAY BE A LADIES' MAN WHO CAN'T HELP FOOLING AROUND...

How should I apologize to the public?

Ugh

Acting without thinking is the guiltiest sin of all...

...

I UNDERSTAND NOW.

I TAKE IT BACK.

WHAT YOU DID IS WHAT A FOREIGNER DOES, AND YOU'RE NOT A LADIES' MAN.

...

WELL... I'M GLAD YOU UNDERSTAND.

What a foreigner does, huh?

But Mr. Tsuruga, please restrain yourself.
Japanese people are not used to that sort of thing!
Uh you're Japanese too, so you should understand.
Please react properly depending on who you're with!
I understand, of course.
I don't...
...kiss all Japanese people...
...
That means...

YOU KISS ANYBODY IF THEY'RE FOR-EIGNERS...
What the heck... so you ARE a ladies'...
I SAID, ONLY PEOPLE I WORK WITH.

BUT YOU'RE GOOD AT LYING...
So you're a ladies'...
I DON'T TELL LIES THAT TRAMPLE A WOMAN'S HEART.

SOME-TIMES YOU'RE TOO NICE FOR NO REASON...
So you're...
WHAT'S WRONG WITH THAT?
A CON MAN IS HANDSOME, NICE, AND A SMOOTH TALKER...
YOU'RE CALLING ME A CROOK?

OH?
SHE'S BACK ON HER FEET...
...
So...
IT WAS NOTHING MUCH.

WHAT WAS THE PROBLEM?
THERE WAS A SLIGHT MISUNDERSTANDING.
IT'S BEEN SOLVED, SO SHE'S ALL RIGHT NOW.
OH, SO IT REALLY WAS NOTHING MUCH.
I worried too much...
HMM...

Well...
I WON'T ASK YOU WHAT THAT MISUNDERSTANDING WAS.

chuckle
THANK YOU.
Excuse me.

THE "MISUNDERSTANDING HAS BEEN SOLVED" ...HUH?

I DIDN'T WANT TO HURT HER...

...SO I TOLD HER...
...THERE WAS NO DESIRE IN THAT KISS...

...BUT SOME-WHERE INSIDE ...
...A SLIGHT SCAR...
... REMAINS IN HER HEART.
...I HOPE...
DOES THAT...

... MAKE ME...
...A BAD GUY...
...WHO TOYS WITH A WOMAN'S HEART?

End of Act 150

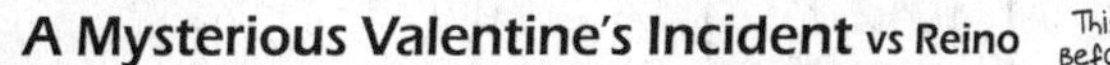

SO... YOU REMEMBERED...

You're so pathetic, chasing me here.

Of course I did. That's why I made the chocolates.

Shut up!

She came after Reino, who disappeared after hearing Ren's name.

Hey! How could you?!
POOR THING!
I mean, poor ME!
THIS IS CUTE.
NO IT'S NOT!
It's not cute at all!
It's about to die!
You're really nuts!
IT'S CUTE...
How bourgeois...
Give it back to me quick!
tug tug
REI-NO.
YOU DO NEED TO COMPLIMENT WOMEN IF YOU WANT TO SCORE...
...BUT YOU'RE COMPLIMENTING HER THE WRONG WAY.
OH?
YOU MUST COMPLIMENT THE WOMAN HERSELF.
Ah...
I SEE...
OF COURSE.
WHAT.
Peek
What're you whispering?! Just give it back quick!
KYOKO.
So...
WHAT ?!

THERE'S ...
...SOME-THING I'VE BEEN WANTING TO TELL YOU...
?
HUH ?
...
I...
...LOVE YOU.
HOW-EVER.

Ms. Mio

THE BEAUTY BORN FROM YOUR DIGNITY AND MYSTERIOUSNESS IS SOMETHING I'VE NEVER SEEN BEFORE.

I PREFER YOU WITH BLACK HAIR AND THE SCARS ON YOUR CHEEK.

SHE WAS A MIRACLE WHO MADE ME FEEL FOR THE FIRST TIME THE BEAUTY OF A LIVING WOMAN.

But look at the way you are now. You look like other boring women, and your aura has faded.

What's happened to you?

IF I DIDN'T POSSESS THE SKILLS TO DETECT YOUR SOUL AND AURA...

...I WOULDN'T HAVE BEEN ABLE TO FIND YOU AGAIN.

WHY WAS KYOKO SO ANGRY WHEN I...
... COMPLIMENTED HER?
YOU COMPLIMENTED THE WAY SHE USED TO BE.
Yeag...
And it was a role she played.
REINO... YOU JUST DON'T GET IT...
DAZED
AND YOU'RE JUST TOO HONEST.
YOU SHOULD ONLY SAY SOMETHING WHEN IT GIVES YOU AN ADVANTAGE.

This episode couldn't be included in the main story. Reino rubbed Kyoko the wrong way with the Grudge Kyoko cell phone strap and his confession of love.

Skip-Beat! End Notes

Everyone knows how to be a fan, but sometimes cool things from other cultures need a little help crossing the language barrier.

Page 59, panel 1: 5,000 yen
About $61 U.S.

Page 86, panel 3: Nio statue
Statues of guardian gods that are placed at temple gates. One is the Agyo (with its mouth open), and the other is the Ungyo (with its mouth closed).

Page 111, panel 2: Hannya
One of the masks used in Noh theater. It represents a female demon or ogre.

Page 146, panel 1: Shota
Short for Shotacon, or Shotaro Complex. An interest in young boys. The opposite is Lolicon, or Lolita Complex.

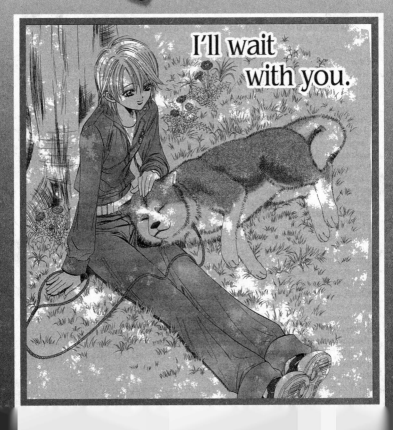

Skip·Beat!

Volume 26

CONTENTS

Skip·Beat!
Act 151: The Most Powerful Emblem

tmp
tmp
tmp
tmp

OH?

SO...
...YOU'RE HERE AT THE AGENCY TODAY TOO?
!
MOOOKOOOOO!

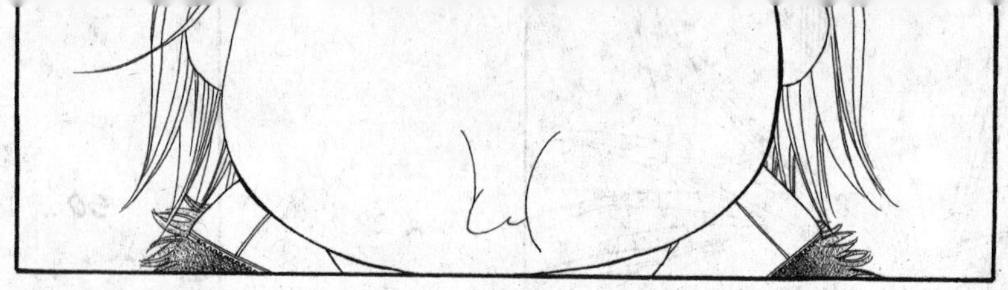

WE HAVEN'T SEEN EACH OTHER IN A WHILE, SO YOU COULD'VE AT LEAST HUGGED ME...
POUT
IT HASN'T BEEN A WHILE.

WE SAW EACH OTHER WHEN WE MADE CHOCOLATES TOGETHER THE OTHER DAY.
!

SO...
...HOW DID THINGS GO, MOKO?
WHAT?

Hio.
WAS HE HAPPY TO GET CHOCO-LATES?
OF COURSE HE'D BE HAPPY...
NO.
HE DIDN'T LOOK PARTICU-LARLY HAPPY.
Come come come. Here here here. Take it, take it, Hio.
S-Sure...
Whaaaat ?!
Obviously.
Well... I forced him to accept them, so I can understand why.
OH.
THEN WAS HE FROWN-ING?
DID HE WRINKLE UP HIS FOREHEAD AND LOOK ANNOYED WHEN YOU GAVE HIM YOUR CHOCOLATES?!
No.
How could you?!
My chocolates didn't upset him that much!
OH...
Hmm... That's no fun.
...
...

WHAT ABOUT YOU?
HMM?
YOU GAVE CHOCOLATES TO EVERYONE.
YEAH.
VM———M
EVERYONE WAS REALLY HAPPY...
...
Everyone?
Uh...
WHAT ABOUT...
...MR. TSURUGA?

WHY'D YOU FREEZE?
S-SO!
MAYBE MR. TSURUGA!

...ACTED LIKE A CHILD AND SULKED...

CUZ HE WAS THE ONLY ONE WHO DIDN'T GET CHOCOLATES FROM HER!

And even made nasty remarks...

I NEVER THOUGHT MR. TSURUGA WOULD DO SOMETHING LIKE THAT, BUT...

...HE WAS HAPPY TOO.

SO HAPPY ...

...THAT I FIND IT IRRITATING EVEN NOW...

DOO-M...

GLOOM...

DARK-NESS

ZAZAT

!

I LEARNED THAT A "THANK YOU" CAN ONLY HARM YOU IF YOU DON'T STICK TO YOUR BOUNDARIES...

PEOPLE SHOULD DO EVERYTHING IN MODERATION ...

...SO THE WORLD CAN BE PEACE-FUL!
LET US PROTECT THE JAPANESE CHARACTER OF NOT BEING BLUNT!
BANZAI!!
Ban-zai to the shy Japan-ese!
WOOOOO!
Be shy for-ever until the world rots away!
My Peace Party Kyoko
UH... SO...
...HE THANKED HER SO MUCH IT FREAKED HER OUT...

...
Hmm~...
Did he...
...KISS HER?
I WOULDN'T BE SURPRISED IF MR. TSURUGA IS A LADY'S MAN.
PEOPLE GET FOOLED BY HIS QUIET, GENTLEMANLY MANNER...
No...
...MAYBE HE'S USING THOSE TRAITS TO HIDE THE FACT THAT HE'S A LADY'S MAN...
Please!
Please cooperate!
Let us be shy and protect this country!
One. Be reserved with thank yous.
Two. Don't touch. No touching.
Ah!
Come on! You look like you're aggressive towards women, but you...
...become a shy boy too!
Yes!
Three. Don't stare.
WELL...
...
...IF HE THANKED HER THAT MUCH, SHE MUST'VE GIVEN HIM SOMETHING.
Enough. I'm ashamed of you.
Hy Heagrh Harhy grh
My Peace Party
It's the Love Me members... Love Me members do strange things like this...
I'M GLAD MY FEARS WERE UNFOUNDED.
MO.
I DON'T MIND YOU BEING A WEIRDO...
...BUT I WISH YOU'D RESTRAIN YOURSELF WHEN I'M WITH YOU.

PEOPLE WILL THINK I'M A WEIRDO TOO.
stomp
COME ON.
I'm not a weirdo.
stomp
AND, AND...
WE'RE NOT WEIRDOS ...
...WE'RE COM-RADES.
WE'RE BOUND BY SOMETHING THAT'S AS STRONG AS A CURSE...
...AND BY A BEAUTIFUL FRIEND-SHIP.
SECTION ME inL.M.Eproduction
THERE'S ONLY TWO OF US.
THE LOVE ME...
SECTION ME inL.M.Eproduction

...MEMBERS...
KA CHAK
THE CURSE BOND IS ENOUGH!
YOU'RE BEING CREEPY!
A beautiful something or whatever!
Really ?
la laa tra laa laaaaa
I'm so happy!
SQUEEZE
Really ...
tra laa laaa tra laa

SKRNCH
SKRNCH
SKRNCH
SKRNCH
SKRNCH
SKRNCH
SKRNCH
SKRNCH
SKRNCH
SKRNCH
SKRNCH
But I'm super-jealous, all right?
No problem! ☆ I can handle it! ♡
Rage Diary
What the hell? Her acting is unnatural, as usual. If you can't act, you should just sing your horrible songs. You're just a success because you're cute. You really piss me off!

M...
Ms. Ama-miya?!
Ah... now I remember...
...there're THREE of us...
.....
WHO... ...IS SHE?
Her aura makes me really uncomfortable...
I JOINED THE LOVE ME SECTION LAST MONTH.
I'M CHIORI AMAMIYA FROM SOFT HAT.
NICE TO MEET YOU.

SOFT HAT?
NEVER HEARD OF IT...
Heh heh
IT'S A SMALL AGENCY...
...SO WHEN I TOLD THEM I WAS QUITTING TO JOIN THE LOVE ME SECTION...

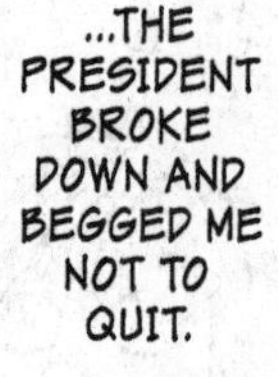
Highest earner
...THE PRESIDENT BROKE DOWN AND BEGGED ME NOT TO QUIT.

SO OUR PRESIDENT TALKED TO THE LME PRESIDENT...
...AND NOW I CAN STAY IN SOFT HAT BUT STILL BE A LOVE ME MEMBER–
HUH?!

Uh...
HOLD IT... DOES THAT MEAN...
...YOU VOLUNTEERED TO BECOME A LOVE ME...
...member?
YES, I DID.
Of course.

SHE'S A WEIRDO!
THIS ONE'S A WEIRDO TOO!
Appalled
Um...
SO, MS. AMAMIYA...

WHAT'RE YOU DOING HERE?

AH...

I'M BEING FORCED TO WRITE A REPORT...

Though I haven't been able to write anything yet.

She's been too busy writing in her Rage Diary.

A REPORT ...?

YES.

AFTER WATCHING ALL THE DRAMAS MICHIKA KAWAGOE HAS STARRED IN.

Three series

BANG

Huh?

...TO THE PRESIDENT.

OH...

THEN HE ASKED ME A QUESTION ...

WHY'RE YOU DOING THAT AT LME?

I JUST CAME HERE TO SAY HELLO...

...AND WHEN I ANSWERED HONESTLY, HE ORDERED ME TO DO THIS.

?

WHAT DID HE ASK YOU ...?

Hey, you're here! How was Valentine's Day...
...Love Me members?
flick
flick
Anaconda
Inner tube?

It's not poisonous, and it's still an adolescent. You don't have to be so scared...
Mr. Takarada will play with you later, Natsuko.
Natsuko
It likes people.
SO?

WHAT DID YOU DO FOR VALEN-TINE'S DAY?

I GAVE HANDMADE CHOCOLATES TO MY CO-STAR.

...ALSO GAVE HANDMADE CHOCOLATES TO PEOPLE I WORK WITH, AND TO THE COUPLE WHO OWNS THE PLACE WHERE I LIVE.

AH.
AND TO MOKO TOO! ♡
We made them together, so I gave them to her the day I made them.
...
Kyah!♡
OHO ...

YOU PARTICIPATED IN AN EVENT FULL OF LOVE, LIKE ORDINARY PEOPLE. WHAT A SURPRISE.
I'm impressed, I'm impressed.
I DIDN'T PARTICIPATE CUZ I **WANTED** TO...
Circumstances **FORCED** me too...

THEN ...

twitch

...YOU MUST HAVE HAD **SOME** FUN.

FUN?
URRRRGH
This must be my chocolates!?
GIVE IT BACK! THEY'RE NOT FOR YOU!
COME ON, YOU DON'T NEED TO WAIT FOR THE PERFECT TIME TO GIVE THEM TO ME.
KANAE, YOU JUST NEED TO SHOVE THEM AT ME AND I'LL ACCEPT THEM.
ARGH
I'M TELLING YOU THEY'RE NOT FOR YOU!
How could you be so stupid?!
I TOLD YOU IT'S ALL RIGHT. JUST GIVE THEM TO ME.
...
...HE GRABBED IT WITH HIS BARE HAND TOO!
!
...BY CHERISHING THIS...
!
URRRGH
...
FLASH
.....
SO...
...WHAT SORT OF DAY WAS VALENTINE'S DAY...
...FOR YOU TWO?

IT WAS A NIGHT-MARISH, EVIL DAY...
...THAT THREAT-ENED MY PEACE AND QUIET!
It was a day that polluted society...
...a day that made the idiots even more stupid!
I'm serious!
I'll tell everyone you're a shota actress

DARN, I COULDN'T HELP ANSWERING HONESTLY.
And Blurting out the truth.
THE PRESIDENT ORDERED US TO WRITE REPORTS TOO, AND THEN JUST LEFT...
Was he taking it out on us?
He seemed offended...
COME ON.
YOU TWO ONLY HAVE TO WRITE ABOUT THE RELATIONSHIP...
...OF THE TWO MAIN CHARACTERS.
MS. AMAMIYA, ISN'T THAT WHAT YOU HAVE TO WRITE TOO?
...
I HAVE...
...TO WRITE ABOUT MICHIKA KAWAGOE HERSELF, WHO GOT CAST CUZ SHE'S CUTE.
HUH?
WHY DO YOU NEED TO WRITE ABOUT THAT?
The President ordered you to, right?
I TOLD YOU, IT'S CUZ I ANSWERED HONESTLY.
That's why I'm being forced to write this report.
AH...
PRESIDENT TAKARADA ASKED ME THE SAME QUESTION.

SO WHAT SORT OF DAY...
...WAS VALENTINE'S DAY FOR YOU?
THREE YEARS AGO ON THIS DAY, MICHIKA KAWAGOE, WHOSE ONLY REDEEMING QUALITY IS BEING CUTE, MADE THE MISTAKE OF APPEARING IN HER FIRST DRAMA!
FEBRUARY 14TH IS THE WORST DAY OF MY LIFE AND I WON'T GET OVER IT!
And she starred in it! How could she?! She's an idol who doesn't know how the world works! She just needs to smile to get everything! I hope she falls to the very bottom of the earth!
AND ...
... WHAT DID YOU...
... SAY?
The worst day and I can't get over it... nope.
...
...

I... I'M SURPRISED YOU WOULD SAY SOMETHING LIKE THAT...
You always write things like that in your diary.
WERE YOU THAT ANGRY...
... ABOUT MICHIKA KAWAGOE?
WELL ...
...YES.

NOT JUST HER, THOUGH.
The worst day of my life that I just can't get over... there's as many of those days as there are people who make it big without having to try hard.
Poisonous aura
SO PRESIDENT TAKARADA REPRIMANDED ME...

"JEALOUSY IS A PROFESSIONAL HAZARD IN A BUSINESS WHERE POPULARITY RULES...

"...BUT YOU CAN'T GROW UNLESS YOU CAN HONESTLY ADMIT THAT SOMEONE ELSE IS TALENTED...

"...EVEN IF THE OTHER PERSON SEEMS LESS CAPABLE THAN YOU."

Ah...

SO...

...SO YOU HAVE TO FIND SOMETHING GOOD ABOUT MICHIKA KAWAGOE'S ACTING FOR YOUR REPORT?

RIGHT.

WHAT AN IMPOSSIBLE ORDER...

WHAT'S SO GOOD ABOUT HER?
RIIIIIGHT?

IT'S PAINFUL WATCHING HER CUZ SHE MAKES IT SO OBVIOUS SHE'S ACTING...
AND HER TEARS JUST NOW WERE OBVIOUSLY EYE DROPS.

EX-ACTLY.
You can fool the viewers, but you can't fool a pro.
THE MORE I LOOK AT HER, THE MORE IRRITATED I GET...

IF YOU CAN'T EVEN CRY, YOU SHOULDN'T BE AN ACTRESS.

YOU ARE SO RIGHT.

THESE TWO...

...ARE GETTING ALONG?

HMM?

RAGE INFERNO
?!
NOOOOO!
HUH?
WHAT?

YOU HAVEN'T MATURED AT ALL AS LOVE ME MEMBERS.
I'M NOT SIMPLY SAD, I'M **FURIOUS.**
MS. MOGAMI, MS. KOTONAMI.
Y-YES ...
Sitting up straight
WHAT HAVE YOU BEEN DOING THIS PAST YEAR?

WELL ...
Um...
I'M SORRY ...
NOTHING IN PARTICULAR...
...BECAUSE I DIDN'T GET ANY ASSIGNMENTS AS A LOVE ME MEMBER...
You fool!
HOW COULD YOU BE SO PASSIVE WHEN YOUR JOB IS TO BE LOVED BY PEOPLE?!

IF JOBS DON'T COME YOUR WAY, GO OUT AND GET THEM!
YOU SEEM TO HAVE FORGOTTEN THAT A LOVE ME MEMBER...
...MUST ANTICIPATE WHAT OTHER PEOPLE WANT AND DO THOSE THINGS WITH LOVE...
...SO THAT THEY'RE IMPRESSED WITH YOU AND LOVE YOU.
YES.
...YOU WANT TO SAY "WE'RE ALREADY ACTRESSES, SO WE DON'T CARE ABOUT THE LOVE ME SECTION ANYMORE."
AM I RIGHT?
sigh
WELL.
JUST AS I EX-PECTED.
...
YOU LOOK LIKE...
JOLT

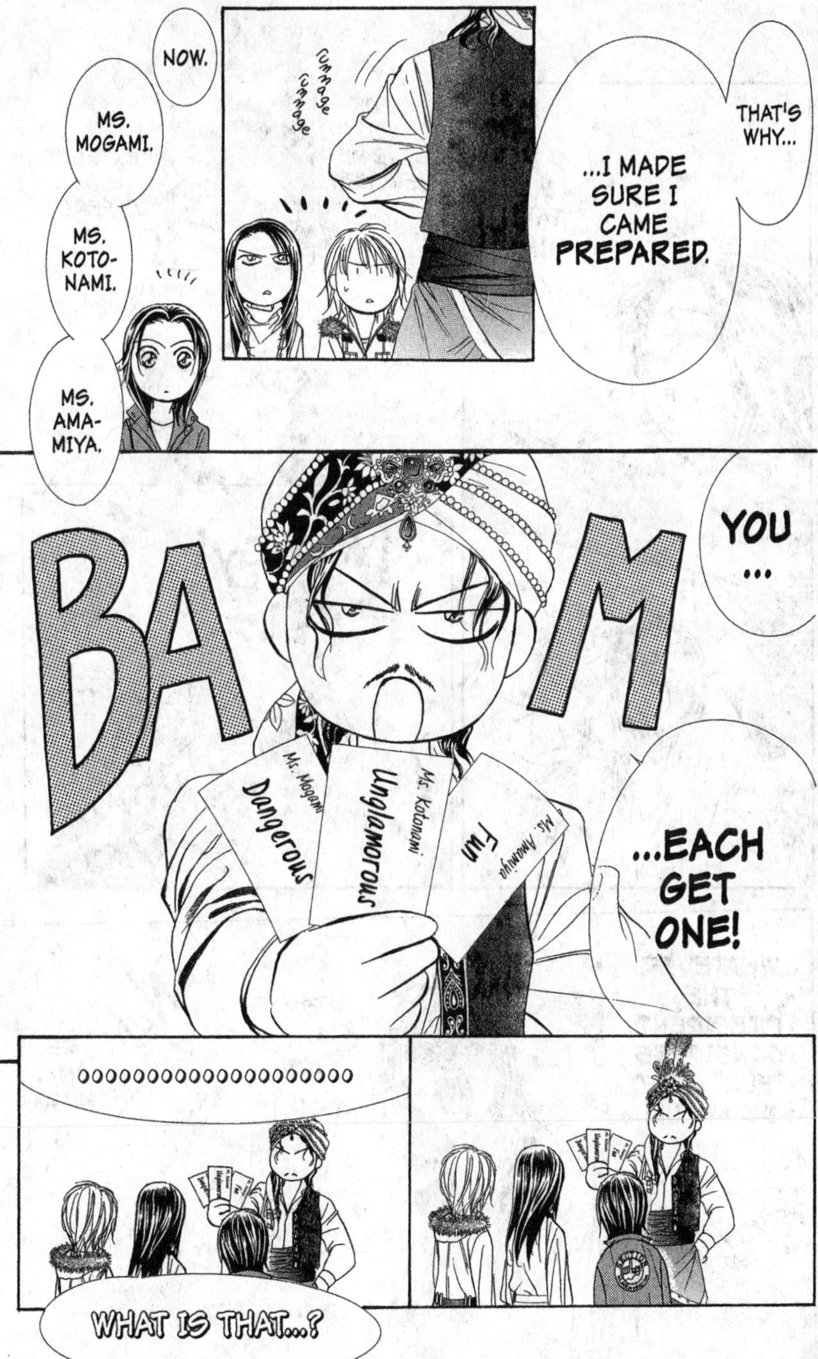
THAT'S WHY...
...I MADE SURE I CAME PREPARED.
rummage rummage
NOW.
MS. MOGAMI.
MS. KOTO-NAMI.
MS. AMA-MIYA.
YOU ...
...EACH GET ONE!
BAM
Ms. Mogami
Dangerous
Ms. Kotonami
Unglamorous
Ms. Amamiya
Fun
OOOOOOOOOOOOOOOOOOOO
WHAT IS THAT...?

EXTREME JOB OFFERS...
...FOR YOU LOVE ME MEMBERS...
...THAT I HAVE SPE-CIALLY SELEC-TED.
No way!
Mine says dangerous!
What do you mean by "unglamor-ous"?!
OH.
I'LL TAKE MINE.
It's fun ♪
Ah!

MS. AMA-MIYA!
No!
STOP RIGHT THERE!
WHATEVER THE PRESIDENT CONSIDERS "FUN" MUST BE AWFUL!
And it's been SPECIALLY SELECTED!

Presideeeent!
I refu~~~se!
I simply refu~~~se!
tmp tmp tmp tmp tmp tmp
...
I refuse.
NO BACKSIES.
WH...
WHAT WAS THAT?
Well...
I DON'T KNOW...
... BUT ...
...WE'LL JUST NOT ACCEPT THE ASSIGNMENTS...
Y-YOU'RE RIGHT.
YEAH ...
Peek

End of Act 151

AJ
YOU...
MAJIMA
...SERI-OUS?
SUKASUKASUKASUKASUKA
Skip·Beat!
Act 152: Violence Mission, Phase 1

...

AH...

THAT'S THE VARIETY SHOW THAT PREMIERED LAST YEAR. ALL THE POPULAR COMEDIANS APPEAR IN IT.

The ratings are amazing.

SOME IDOLS AND TALENTOS APPEAR TOO, AND THE VIEWERS LOVE THE VARIOUS BATTLES.

Ah!

"This Show Will Really Make You Feel Good"!

I've heard about it, but I haven't seen it.

But I see lots of posters for it at Fuji.

...

WHY DO I...

...HAVE TO MINGLE WITH ALL THOSE COMEDIANS...
Ms. Amamiya
Fun
This Show Will Really Make You Feel Good
...WHEN I'M ALREADY PLAYING A NASTY ROLE IN A DRAMA?
IF I APPEAR IN A COMEDY SHOW, PEOPLE MIGHT THINK I'M JUST FLIGHTY AND STUPID.
OH...
...BUT...

...I HEAR ALL THE TIME ABOUT IDOLS AND TALENTOS WITH EDGY IMAGES GETTING POPULAR BY APPEARING IN VARIETY SHOWS.
!
MS. AMAMIYA! HERE'S YOUR CHANCE!

HUH?

IT'S AN OPPORTUNITY NOT TO GET STUCK WITH YUMIKA'S BAD IMAGE!

IF VIEWERS SEE YOU ACT GOOFY AND PLAYFUL ON THE VARIETY SHOW...

...THEY WON'T THINK YOU'RE LIKE YOUR CHARACTER.

AND...

...BY HAVING THE VIEWERS REALIZE THAT YUMIKA IS JUST A CHARACTER...

...YOU CAN PROVE YOUR ACTING ABILITY AS WELL!

Wow, the President thought it through that far?!

Much respect

NO... I THINK HE SIMPLY CHOSE IT BECAUSE IT LOOKS FUN...

...

YOU GOTTA TAKE ADVANTAGE OF THIS OPPORTUNITY...

...MS. AMAMIYA—

NO.

WHA ...?
I SAID NO.
NO MATTER HOW BIG THE REWARDS ...
...I DO NOT WANT TO BE ON THE SET OF THAT SHOW!
Ah
YOU'RE PROBABLY WORRYING OVER NOTHING, BUT COMEDIANS DO USE THEIR PASTS AND HEARTACHES FOR LAUGHS ...
I can under-stand how you feel...
It's not that I hate variety shows!
I DON'T WANT TO BECOME THEIR TARGET!
I DON'T WANT TO BE WITH ALL THOSE COMEDIANS!
I HATE COMEDIANS, CUZ THEY THINK THEY CAN SAY AND DO ANYTHING FOR LAUGHS!
YOUR PAST...
I see...
MAYBE MS. AMAMIYA ...
...IS THINKING ABOUT HER PAST AS A CHILD ACTRESS.

I'M GONNA APPEAR IN A SAMURAI DRAMA.

I'M AN ORPHAN FROM A SAMURAI FAMILY WHO FOLLOWS AROUND A RONIN WHO SAVED HER LIFE.

What's with that setting?! Am I a stalker?!

It's unglamorous, clammy and damp!

I want to go "ARGH!" at a woman like that!

But I don't envy her...

THE DAUGHTER OF A SAMURAI FAMILY MEANS SHE'S A RICH YOUNG LADY...

I have issues with this...

...BUT IT'S AN OPPORTUNITY TO ACT, AND I CAN'T AFFORD TO COMPLAIN ABOUT MY ROLES.

pout pout

...

SO THAT MEANS...

...MY ASSIGNMENT IS THE EASIEST.

YOU'RE GONNA PICK UP A GUEST FOR THE PRESIDENT, WHO HAS TO DO SOMETHING ELSE.

YEAH.

Ms. Mogami

Dangerous

WHO KNOWS, THOUGH? YOUR ASSIGNMENT IS "DANGEROUS," AND THE GUEST IS THE PRESIDENT'S GUEST.
THEY COULD BE REALLY DANGEROUS.
Come on~...
THE PRESIDENT IS OUTRAGEOUS...
...BUT HE WON'T REALLY MAKE A FRAIL GIRL GO PICK UP SOMEONE DANGEROUS.

I WONDER ABOUT THAT...
OH.
I SHOULD GO PICK THEM UP NOW.
I need to be at Tokyo Station by 3.
SEE YOU MOKO, MS. AMAMIYA.
chak
THERE'S NO WAY YOU CAN SAY "NO" TO THE PRESIDENT...
WELL ...
...
I'LL MANAGE.
But I won't be working on it for a while.
...YOU HATE IT.
...SO DO YOUR BEST WITH YOUR ASSIGNMENTS EVEN IF...
Yeah.
SEE YOU!
THE PRESIDENT IS SCHEMING SOMETHING, BUT GO FOR IT!
UH...
SHE'S SMILING LIKE IT HAS NOTHING TO DO WITH HER...
As if she's not worried at all...
BUT I THINK HER JOB, WHICH SOUNDS THE EASIEST ...

...IS THE ONE THE PRESIDENT SCHEMED ON THE MOST.
grin
WELL.
I GUESS...
...I'LL GO HOME NOW.
Hmm hmm
la la
After playing with Natsuko one more time! ♡
Yeah!
Natsuko

WELCOME
Mr. CAIN HEEL
Blah
Blah

MR. CAIN HEEL...
... HASN'T ARRIVED YET...
Blah Blah
LME PRODUCTIO
Love Me signs
WELCOME Mr. CAIN HEEL
stare stare
stare
Blah Blah
I'M SURE HE'LL NOTICE ME, SINCE ALL THIS IS SO GAUDY.
Am I at the right exit?
IF I CAN'T GREET HIM, I'LL HAVE WORN MY LOVE ME UNIFORM FOR NOTHING.
GRAB
!
Oh!
HE'S HERE?!
WEL-
HEY... WHAT SORT OF ADVER-TISING IS THIS?
I will not have that flashy pink disrupting traffic.
COME TO THE POLICE BOX RIGHT NOW.

SLAM
We lost her.
She ran away so fast!
She must be working for a crime syndicate!
In a way, he's right
Pant pant
wheeze wheeze
Pant pant
wheeze wheeze
I-I almost got ar-rested!
E-excuse me.
Please... please drive...
Of course.
He looks plenty suspicious, cuz he works for Lory.
Nod
Quick!
Sheesh!
flip
Mr. Cain Heel still hasn't arrived yet!
bip bip
Presi-deeeeent!
Hmm?

WHAT?
A phone call from Ms. Mogami.
OH.
PUT HER THROUGH.
Yes sir.
SPLASH
SPLASH SPLASH
The pool in the LME employee gym
He was still playing with Natsuko.
beep
OH MS. MOGAMI.
SOMETHING WRONG?
Um.
President, excuse me for calling.
I don't know what to do.
HUH? WHAT? DID SOMETHING HAPPEN?
I haven't been able to find him...
HUH?
I haven't been able to pick up Mr. Cain Heel.
He hasn't showed up at Tokyo Station, and it's already past 3:00.
TOKYO STATION?

Ah.
Of course he's not there.
I forgot to tell you.
Cuz I changed the meeting place.
Huh?!
Huh?!
Yeah, yeah.
The new meeting place...
...is in front of the Hachiko statue at Shibuya.
WHAAAT?!
THE HACHIKO ...
...statue?!
Wh ...
Why ...
Did you...
...pick that place?
Huh?
Cuz that's one of the prime spots to meet up.
I figured I should go there at least once, since I live in Tokyo.
SO IT WOULD'VE LOOKED ...
...LIKE THIS?
Faithful Dog Hachiko
When's he coming? When's he coming?
How unnatural...
AT LEAST ONCE?
R-RIGHT ...

WHY DID HE NEED TO DO THIS FOR AN OVERSEAS GUEST?!
Please choose the time and location!
AND HAVEN'T YOU EVER WAITED FOR SOMEONE WHEN YOU WERE YOUNG?!
Near the Hachiko statue!
You were born in Tokyo and grew up here...
agony
suffering
Ah...
I WANT TO COM-PLAIN...
...BUT WHAT YOUR BOSS SAYS GOES! I MUST SMILE AND SAY YES!
Kyoko, a typical Japanese working stiff
Y-YOU'RE RIGHT.
H-Heh heh...
TH-THEN I'LL HEAD OVER THERE RIGHT AWAY...
Ah...
...thanks.
UM...
Uh...
THERE'S SOMETHING I'D LIKE TO ASK FIRST...
What is it?
Will you tell me...
...what Mr. Heel looks like?
SPLASH
I want to make sure I can find him, even if there're a couple of foreigners around...
AH.
NOT TO WORRY.
YOU'LL KNOW IT'S HIM RIGHT AWAY.
squelch
squelch

He'll look like a yakuza.
HUH?
WHAT?
PRESIDENT—
UM... U...
Ah.
Yeah yeah.
He's very considerate, and does everything so properly you'll be impressed...
...so don't be late.
He's actually hot-blooded though...
...so he may casually greet a girl with his fist.
Y...

YOU MEAN HE'S FUSSY, HIGHLY STRUNG, SHORT-TEMPERED, AND VIOLENT!
Don't make those characteristics sound so positive!
Come on.
No problem, no problem.
I changed our meeting time too...
...to 4.
GRAB
15:45
15 minutes left
NOOOOOOOOOOOO!
I don't wanna be beat u~~p!

YOU FOOL.
MO— I TOLD YOU.
YOUR ASSIGNMENT IS "DANGEROUS" AND THE GUEST IS THE PRESIDENT'S GUEST...
...SO HE MAY REALLY BE DANGER-OUS.
HE USED ME AS A PUNCHING BAG THREE SECONDS AFTER WE MET...
I danced in the air 7.5 times, so fast I didn't even get to see the Hachiko Statue.
sob sob
whimper whimper
weep weep
I'm hurting... I'm hurting... Moko...
Comfort meeeeeee.
MO.
ALL RIGHT.

wave
stroke stroke
Now
Pain, pain, go away.
Ah...
I... I'm... so... happy...
Oooh...
I'D...
...LOOOOOOVE THAT...
OOH... NOW THAT I THINK ABOUT IT, SEEING THE HACHIKO STATUE BACKFLIP SEEMS LIKE NOTHING...
It's just an amazing dog...
th-thump th-thump
excited excited
サロンパフ

LET'S GO!
To where the amazing dog is!
I'M HALF AN HOUR LATE, SO MR. HEEL MUST BE FEROCIOUSLY ANGRY!
I DON'T CARE!
NOW!
MAKE ME...
...HAPPY IN THREE SECONDS!

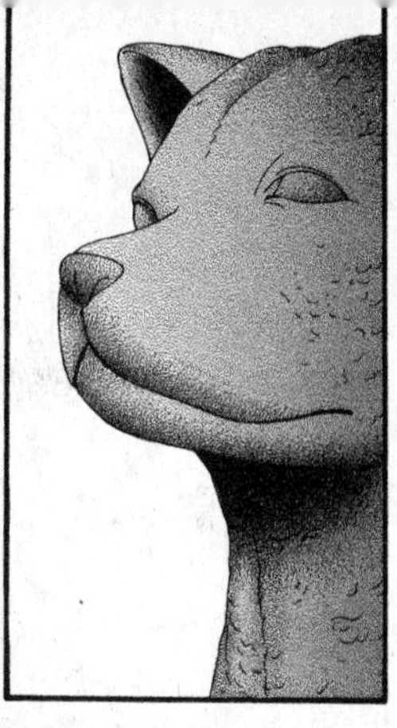

Blah

Blah

Blah

Blah

HUH? MAYBE HE LEFT CUZ HE GOT TIRED OF WAITING?

I feel relieved, But I'm also disappointed.

HE SOUNDS AWFULLY IMPATIENT ...

wander

...SO MAYBE HE WENT OFF TO SEE THE PRESIDENT?

fwip
HUH?
murmur
murmur
murmur
銀座線 渋谷駅
murmur
murmur
murmur
THERE ARE...
...A LOT OF WEIRDOS AROUND HERE...
murmur
...BUT SOMETHING'S DIFFERENT ABOUT HIM...
HE'S NOT NORMAL... I DON'T KNOW... HIS AURA'S DIFFERENT...
...
C...
gulp
THAT MAN...

COULD IT BE?
... MUST'VE ...
STOMP STOMP
STOMP
STOMP
STOMP
KRUSH
CRUNCH
CRUNCH
CRUNCH
... KILLED ...

...ONE OR TWO PEOPLE ...

...FOR SURE...
S.E.C.T.
in L.M.E pro
...
...
I...

IS...

...THAT MAN...

...THE ONE?

Maybe...?

WHA ...?

NO NO, DON'T GIVE UP, KYOKO.

Never Give up!

sway sway

trudge trudge

IF YOU LOOK AROUND, HE MUST BE HERE.

A JAPANESE-BRITISH MAN.

And...

...A MAN WHO LOOKS LIKE A YAKUZA ...

And a man who looks fussy, short-tempered and violent.
sob sob
weep
whimper whimper
THAT MUST BE HIM!

Ugh...
THE HACHIKO STATUE MAY NOT EVEN HAVE A CHANCE TO BACKFLIP...
sob

I'D DIE AND GO TO HEAVEN BEFORE HACHIKO COULD DANCE IN THE AIR...

BUT... I CAN'T HELP IT...

IT'S MY FAULT I WAS LATE...
WELL, IT WASN'T MY FAULT...
...BUT MY BOSS'S MISTAKE IS MY MISTAKE ...
SWF
SO I MUST ...
...RISK MY LIFE AND APOLOGIZE HERE!
ALL RIGHT!
I'LL BE BRAVE.
I'LL BE SINCERE.
NO MATTER HOW FIERY HIS TEMPER IS...
...I'LL LOOK HIM IN THE EYE AND SAY SORRY!
HE'S NOT A BEAST THAT CAN'T COMMUNI-CATE!
NO.
HE'S GOT A BODY THAT'S BEEN WELL TRAINED.
I CAN TELL THAT EVEN WITH ALL THOSE CLOTHES.

EVEN IF EVERYONE HERE...

...ATTACKED HIM AT ONCE...

...HE'D...

...CUT THEM ALL DOWN WITH HIS LONG ARMS AND LEGS.

YES...

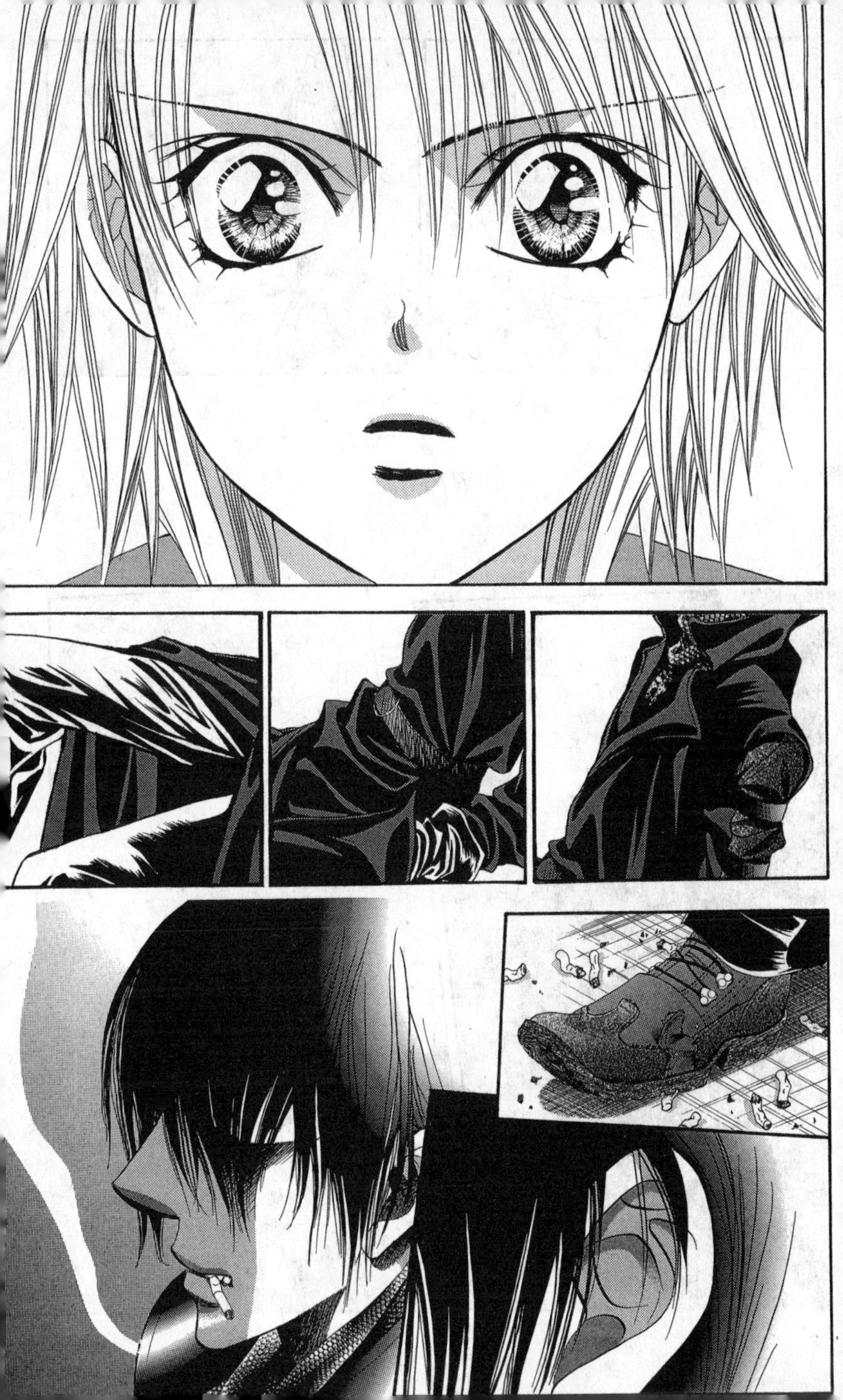

WHA?!
HEY ...
Hey you!
SWAY
SWF

End of Act 152

Skip·Beat!
Act 153: Violence Mission, Phase 1.5

WH...

What's she doing?!
She's approaching someone who looks cranky and evil...
chatter chatter
gasp gasp
And she's...

...wearing a color that rubs people the wrong way...
Ah sheesh, she looks like she's asking people to punch her!
She's suicidal. Someone call the police!

...

YOU'RE ...

...MR. TSURUGA ...
... AREN'T YOU?

.....

...
MR. TSURUGA?
IS...
zat
...IT...

...REALLY YOU?

grit
.....
crunch
jolt
spit
tak
CRUSH

SECTION

THUD

...
SHUUU
...
...

FLAP
fwip
snap
Peek
He only stepped over her.
sway
sway
NOOOOOO
SCURRY
SCURRY

Blah
Blah
Blah
Blah

Blah
Blah
Blah
Blah
UH...

MY FIN-GERS ...
...ARE FINALLY GETTING WARM AGAIN...
It's been 15 minutes since she collapsed.

Faithful Dog Hachiko

MY HEART'S ...
th-thump
th-thump

... BEAT-ING...
th-thump
th-thump
...AGAIN...

...I THINK...
Ha
AH, GOOD. I THINK I CAN STAND UP NOW...
The first time, she was like a new-born calf.

IT FELT...

...LIKE...
...ALL THE BLOOD...
...IN MY BODY...

...WAS SUCKED OUT...
...AT ONCE...
...FROM A WOUND THAT WASN'T...
...EVEN VISIBLE.
clench
SOMETHING'S WRONG WITH ME...

HOW...
...COULD I MISTAKE A DANGEROUS-LOOKING GUY LIKE THAT FOR MR. TSURUGA?
...WITH THE MR. TSURUGA SCALE※ IN MY HEAD.
※ The Mr. Tsuruga scale is based on the detailed data and molds Kyoko uses to make the super-realistic Ren Tsuruga dolls.
ALL THE PARTS OF THE HEAD MATCHED.
THE RATIO OF HEAD TO WHOLE BODY.
THE RATIO OF TORSO TO LOWER BODY.
THE RATIO OF UPPER ARM TO LOWER ARM.
THE RATIO OF THIGH TO CALF.
THE ANGLE AND FORMATION OF THE SHOULDER AND WAIST.
BUT...
...HE MATCHED...
...PERFECTLY...
THE MUSCLES YOU CAN SENSE EVEN WHEN HE'S WEARING CLOTHES.
The biceps muscle...
The greater pectoral muscle, the external abdominal oblique muscle, the trapezius...
Now the data is about his flesh
AND THE BONES THAT MAKE THEM POSSIBLE...
The grand line from the cervical vertebra to the lumbar spine...
The perfect guardian of humerus. The acrominon of the shoulder blade...
Now the data is about bones that you can't even see
IN ANY CASE...
A... JAPANESE GUY LIKE THAT...
No...
HE'S LIKE A SPACE ALIEN, WITH A BODY LIKE THAT.

AND I THOUGHT THERE WASN'T ANYBODY ELSE WHO HAD EXACTLY THE SAME SORT OF BODY...
trudge
trudge
trudge
trudge
I'M GLAD...
...HE WASN'T MR. TSURUGA...
BUT...
WELL... MR. TSURUGA IS SCARY WHEN HE GETS REALLY ANGRY...
So much I cry and beg for mercy...
but...
HE'S NOT LIKE THAT MAN...
...WHO USES "BLOOD-THIRST" AS ARMOR AND WEAPON.
I COULDN'T FEEL ANY "HEART" IN HIM...
...AND...

...MR. TSURUGA ISN'T LIKE THAT...

HOW COULD YOU WALK AROUND IN SOMETHING LIKE THAT?
I'D STAY AT HOME.
Chuckle
YEAH.
Poor girl.
SHE'S GOT BAD TASTE IN CLOTHES, AND SHE'S STUPID...
OH?
Blah Blah
tmp tmp tmp

WHERE DID THAT PINK WEIRDO GO?

......
shake shake
Mfft.
Gnh.
BFFT GNH
Mfft gnh.
Gnh.
jerk
...
...SORRY.
I'M SORRY.
I'M SORRY.
I'M SORRY.
I'M SORRY I AP-PROACHED YOU.
I'M SORRY I MADE A MISTAKE.

I'M SORRY I THOUGHT YOU WERE SOMEONE ELSE.
A pill bug
I'M SORRY FOR WEARING THIS EYESORE UNIFORM.
...
MS. MOGAMI...
I'M SORRY I BELONG IN A STUPID-SOUNDING DEPARTMENT LIKE THE LOVE ME SECTION.
I'M SORRY OUR PRESIDENT IS SUCH A WEIRDO.
MS. MOGAMI, CALM DOWN.
Pat
Pat
YOU DON'T NEED TO BE SO SCARED.
Pat
Pat
Peek

BINGO.

Heh

YES?
MR. TSURU—
Mrmph!
YEAH YEAH, SORRY. DON'T RAISE YOUR VOICE.
...
I'M ON A TOP-SECRET MISSION.

waft
waft
fuuu

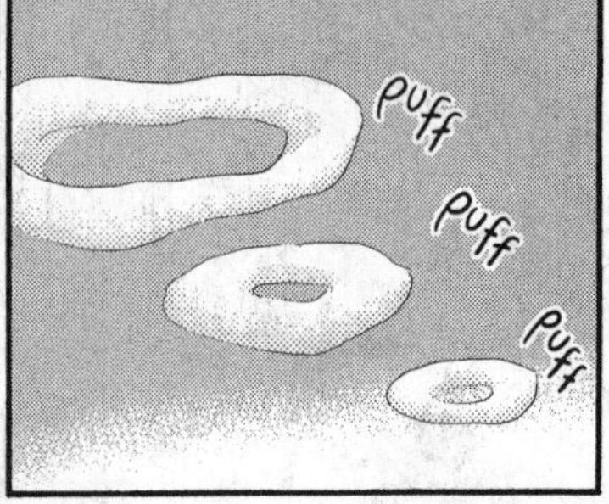
puff
puff
puff

fuuu
peek

ARE YOU...
...
...
poit
... STUPID?

HOW COULD YOU REVEAL YOUR IDENTITY?
IT'S TOP SECRET. THE MYSTERY ACTOR, CAIN HEEL, STARRING AS B.J.
I KNOW...
...BUT I'M SURE MS. MOGAMI WILL KEEP HER MOUTH SHUT...

...AND I FELT GUILTY THAT I SCARED HER.
OHO, OHO.
SO THAT'S HOW YOU'RE JUSTIFYING IT.
YOU MUST'VE SCARED HER SO MUCH YOU COULDN'T IGNORE HER.
Well, I can understand. He's a man in love.
AND...
...ALTHOUGH I DIDN'T EXPECT REN TO REVEAL HIS IDENTITY HIMSELF...
...I WAS GOING TO EXPLAIN EVERYTHING TO MS. MOGAMI EVENTUALLY.
SO SOONER OR LATER, SHE'D HAVE KNOWN...
...
MS. MOGAMI.

YES?
SOOO...
REN'S TOLD YOU WHAT'S GOING ON, RIGHT?
UH...
...MOST OF IT, YES...
HMM...
THEN...
...I'D LIKE TO TAKE THIS OPPOR-TUNITY...
...TO ASK YOU...
...TO ACCEPT ANOTHER JOB...
WHA...?

THIS CASTING CALL TODAY.
IF REN HADN'T REVEALED HIS IDENTITY...
...I THINK HE'D HAVE FOOLED YOU, SO I'M NOT WORRIED...
...THAT OTHER PEOPLE WILL FIND OUT WHO HE REALLY IS.

HOWEVER...

...IT'S SAFER IF SOMEONE WHO KNOWS THE TRUTH IS BY HIS SIDE...

...CUZ I CAN'T HAVE YASHIRO TAKE CARE OF CAIN HEEL.
Ah.
YOU'RE RIGHT...
Ha
UH.
I GET IT.

I'LL FILL IN FOR MR. YASHIRO!
Let me handle it! I've done it before, so Kyoko Mogami will do a perfect job!
Pat
...
NO.
THAT'S NOT IT.

HUH?

I'D LIKE ...
...YOU...

...STARTS NOW...

A "DANGEROUS" JOB.
YOUR REAL JOB...
grin

...TO BE REN'S GOOD-LUCK CHARM.

...MS. MOGAMI...

End of Act 153

Skip·Beat!
Act 154: Violence Mission, Phase 2

A GOOD-LUCK CHARM

shing

TRAFFIC SAFETY

shing

Perfect health

UH.

HAPPY FAMILY

I DON'T THINK THIS IS WHAT THE PRESIDENT MEANT...
Well...
I CAN MAKE A GOOD-LUCK CHARM TO WARD OFF EVIL...
shing
MY PRAYERS COME TRUE
rustle
rustle
BUT.

...LIKE THIS.
NO...
Perfect health

IMAGINE REN TSURUGA KEEPING A GOOD-LUCK CHARM...

I-I-I-IT DOESN'T SUIT HIM AT ALL...
I mean, what the heck?!
WHAT IS IT EXACTLY? A MISMATCH? INCOM-PATIBLE? WATER AND OIL?
I THOUGHT I KNEW MYSELF PRETTY WELL...

...BUT WHAT I LOVE DOESN'T SUIT MR. TSURUGA ONE BIT...

OH!
UH.

NOW I'M GETTING REALLY WORRIED!
About his Birthday Gift...
DID HE LIKE IT?
OR WAS HE UPSET BECAUSE IT WASN'T SOMETHING HE'D USE?
Disappointed
OR MAYBE HE GOT EMBARRASSED WHEN HE TOOK IT OUT IN PUBLIC!
AH... YES!
NO!
Well, YES!
EVEN I ASKED HIM TO OPEN IT AT HOME ALONE BECAUSE I WAS EMBARRASSED ABOUT HAVING HIM OPEN IT IN FRONT OF ME!
I WASN'T EMBAR-RASSED ABOUT WHAT I'D GIVEN HIM.
I WAS EMBARRASSED ABOUT HAVING HIM OPEN IT IN THE REHEARSAL ROOM, WHICH WAS FULL OF EXPENSIVE-LOOKING GIFTS!
A pile of Gifts wrapped in designer wrapping paper.
And more in the Back.
BUT NOW...

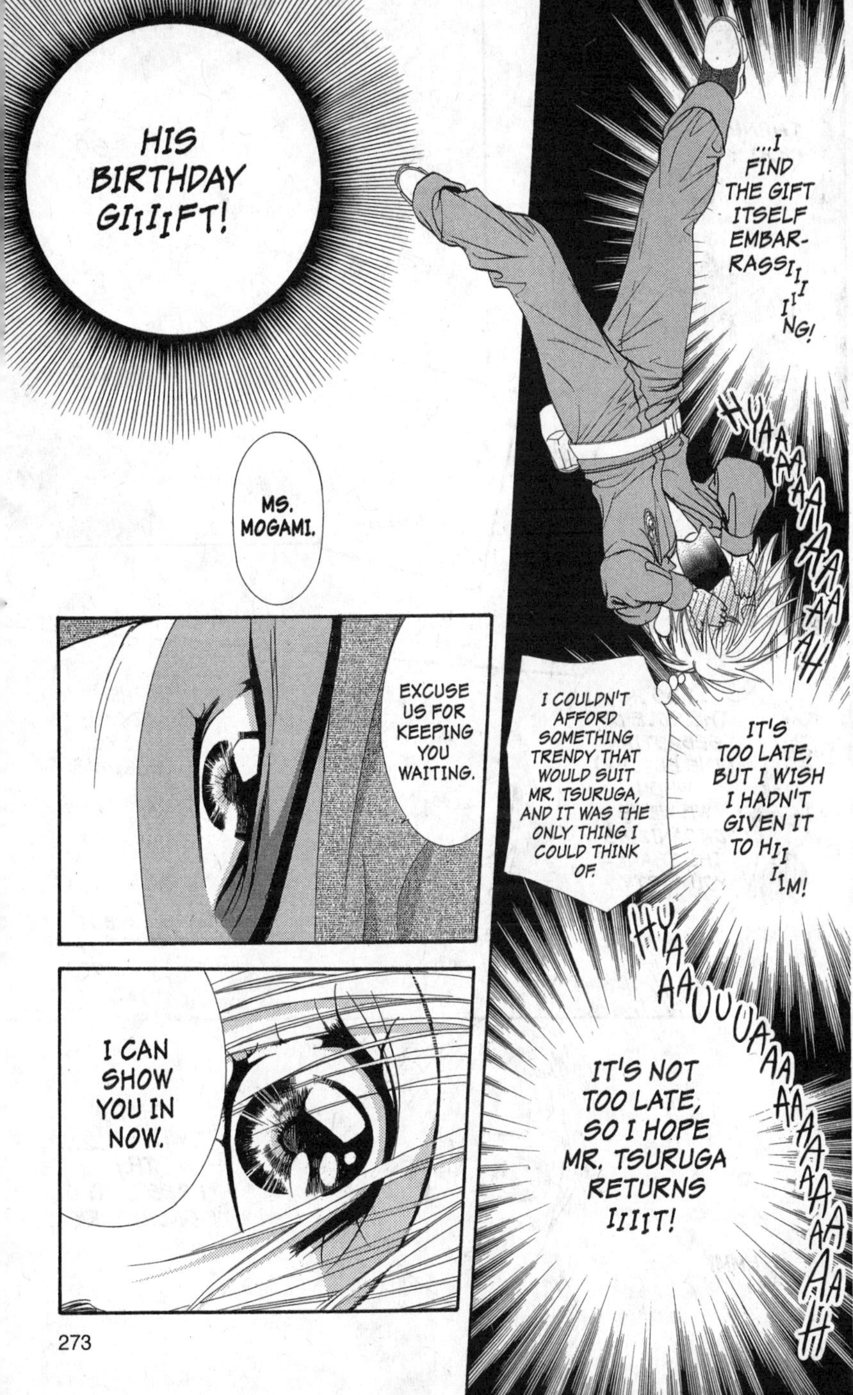
...I FIND THE GIFT ITSELF EMBARRASSIIIING!
HYAAAAAAAAAAAH
I COULDN'T AFFORD SOMETHING TRENDY THAT WOULD SUIT MR. TSURUGA, AND IT WAS THE ONLY THING I COULD THINK OF.
IT'S TOO LATE, BUT I WISH I HADN'T GIVEN IT TO HIIIM!
HYAAAUUUAAAAAAAAAAAAAAH
IT'S NOT TOO LATE, SO I HOPE MR. TSURUGA RETURNS IIIIT!
HIS BIRTHDAY GIIIIFT!
MS. MOGAMI.
EXCUSE US FOR KEEPING YOU WAITING.
I CAN SHOW YOU IN NOW.

SO MAY I?
Ladies Room ♀
Fried shrimp
THIS WAY, PLEASE.
Th—
THANK YOU...
THIS MAN...
...WAS IN THE ROLE OF SEBASTIAN (THE BUTLER) WHEN WE WERE ORGANIZING THE THANK-YOU PARTY...
Don't know his real name
HE LOOKS VERY SERIOUS ...
Uh...
OKAY.
OVER THERE, PLEASE.
...BUT HE'S A WEIRDO TOO.
THAT'S WHY HE'S THE PRESIDENT'S SECRETARY ...
HMM?

AH.
H-i-i-i-i-i-!♡
SO YOU'RE KYOKO?
NICE TO MEET YOU.
I'M JELLY WOODS, AND I'LL BE TAKING CARE OF YOU TODAY.
HUH?? UH...
N-NICE TO MEET YOU TOO...
I DON'T QUITE UNDER-STAND WHAT'S GOING ON.
What?
OH, NO.
Really?
DARLING HASN'T EXPLAINED IT TO YOU YET?
Huh?

"DARLING"?
Wh-Who does she mean??
Sheesh, all right.
I DON'T MIND. I'VE KNOWN HIM FOR A LONG TIME...
...AND I KNOW HOW OUT-RAGEOUS HE CAN BE.
SECTION
Outrageous...
N-No...
NO, NO...
BUT TO ACT THAT WAY TOWARDS A YOUNG GIRL...
How could he?
grumble
A LOVELY WOMAN LIKE THIS CAN'T BE...
A YOUNG GIRL...
Uh... But you're young too...
AREN'T WE ABOUT THE SAME AGE? SHE CAN'T BE MORE THAN A FEW YEARS OLDER THAN ME.
...WHEN YOU GET USED TO DARLING'S OUTRAGEOUS-NESS, IT'S REALLY FUN...
Oh...
BUT...
O...
OH...
...AND NOW I'LL PROVE IT TO YOU.
SECTION
FWIP

I'M JELLY WOODS.
PEOPLE CALL ME "THE WITCH OF THE BEAUTY INDUSTRY."
A...A witch?!
th-thump
BY MY NAME, I SHALL...
... CHANGE YOUR LIFE...
SHK

...IN FIVE MINUTES.

YOU'RE BEING RUDE.
YOU ASSUME I'M ALWAYS COMING UP WITH EVIL SCHEMES.
I'M NOT "ASSUMING." YOU ALWAYS ARE, AND THAT'S WHY I HAVE MY DOUBTS.

And Ren would "pass" if he could get to Lory's place without revealing his true identity.
TODAY YOU TOLD ME YOU WERE HAVING SOMEONE I KNOW PRETTY WELL FROM THE ACTORS SECTION PICK ME UP...
...BUT YOU HAD MS. MOGAMI COME GET ME. THAT IS SO SUSPICIOUS.

Hm Ph.

OF COURSE I DID IT ON PURPOSE.

I'M TRAINING YOU SO THAT YOU WON'T PANIC WHEN SOMETHING UNEXPECTED HAPPENS, SO YOU CAN KEEP IN CHARACTER AS CAIN HEEL NO MATTER WHAT.
I'M TOTALLY LYING.
SO TODAY'S REHEARSAL INCLUDED A DISASTER DRILL.
THAT'S TRUE...
WHEN ...

...I SAW THAT SHOCKING PINK OUT OF THE CORNER OF MY EYE, I THOUGHT "NO WAY"...
...AND ALMOST LOOKED UP. I ALMOST BLEW IT.
Cain Heel
Quiet, short-tempered, highly strung (around everyone except his sister), smokes a lot, and moves slowly when he's not working.
SO I GUESS IT DID WORK AS TRAINING.
DIDN'T IT?
Moreover...
YOU WERE ABLE TO FOOL SOMEONE EVEN AFTER THEY REALIZED WHO YOU REALLY WERE.
twitch
BY THE WAY.
You lost in an instant.
HOW'D SHE FIGURE IT OUT?
...
WELL...
... UM...
...
WHAT.
Why don't you just say it?
WAS IT RELATED TO HER FEELINGS FOR YOU?
NO... NOT AT ALL...
I WASN'T JUST SUR-PRISED...
...
...I WAS TERRI-FIED...
Your body parts, the ratios, your flesh, your bones.
So excited
explaining it to him.

I DIDN'T LIKE IT AT ALL THAT SHE RECOGNIZED ME THAT WAY...
What did she mean by "my bones"?
...
PERFECT VISION?
≈Perfect pitch
...I WASN'T EXPECTING...
...anything love-related from her.
Since she's our first Love Me member.
NO.
HOWEVER...
...THAT EXTRAORDINARY REASON...
...MEANS THAT SHE'S BEEN WATCHING REN...
...VERY...
...CLOSELY...
...THIS MISSION...
...IS WORTHWHILE...
Heh
I THINK...
...FOR MS. MOGAMI AS WELL...
Darliiing.

I'm done!
clip
clop
clip
OH, AL-READY?
SORRY, DARLING.
HMM?
...IN ALL BLACK, SO SHE MATCHES CAIN HEEL...
AT FIRST, I WAS GONNA DO LIKE YOU SAID...
...BUT WHEN I ACTUALLY STARTED WORKING ON KYOKO, I GOT OTHER IDEAS...
...SO SHE LOOKS A BIT DIFFER-ENT NOW.
OHO?
...
BUT I THINK SHE REALLY LOOKS LIKE SETSUKA.
So please forgive me.
HMM...
...
WHAT'RE YOU TALKING ABOUT?

HMM ?
WHO'S SETSU-KA?
HEY... PRESI-DENT?
SO?
SHE WAS FOLLOW-ING ME...
...BUT SHE MUST'VE GOTTEN SCARED.
AH.
YOU CALL HER "SETSU", ALL RIGHT?
WHERE IS SHE HIDING?
WHAT ?
HUH ?
OH ?!
I TOLD HER NOT TO BE SHY, CUZ SHE LOOKS CUTE.
WELL, LET'S TAKE A LOOK.
DASH
KYOKO!
HEY, HOLD ON THERE...

YOU DRESSED HER UP SO SHE'S SCARED AND SHY?!
NO, I DIDN'T.
NO NEED TO RAISE YOUR EYEBROWS AT ME.
I...
I DIDN'T ...
...RAISE MY EYE-BROWS.
Sure, sure you didn't.
WELL, IT'S VERY DIFFERENT ...
...FROM THE THINGS SHE LOVES, FROM THE THINGS THAT STRIKE A CHORD WITH HER...

IT'S SOMETHING SHE HASN'T COME IN CONTACT WITH IN HER DAY-TO-DAY LIFE...
...SO SHE PROBABLY FEELS LOST BECAUSE SHE'S NOT USED TO IT.
Ah.
Found you!
Kyoko, what're you doing? Come out quick.
D...
DO I REALLY HAVE TO GO OUT LIKE THIS...?
Dressed like this...
fidget
KYOKO.
THIS IS YOUR JOB.
ARE YOU...
...GOING TO ABANDON YOUR ROLE...
...BECAUSE OF THE WAY YOU'RE DRESSED?

DON'T WORRY.
SHE'LL FORGET ABOUT HER EMBARRASSMENT...
...ONCE SHE'S IN HER ROLE.
?!
IF SHE'S...
...A REAL ACTRESS.
...
ONCE SHE'S IN HER ROLE?
PRESIDENT, WHAT'RE YOU MAKING HER DO?
WHAT DO YOU MEAN BY MY "GOOD-LUCK CHARM"?!
HMM?
WHAT?
LOOK.

TMP
jang
tmp
tmp
tmp

TMP

TUNK

.....
OH HEY, YOU LOOK GOOD.
Ms. Mogami.
You look hard and cute like that.
.....
Speechless
dazed
FROZEN
FROZEN
ISN'T SHE?
I think I did a great job.
She managed to use her Guts to walk and stand like Natsu.
THIS IS GOOD ENOUGH.
SO HERE'S...
...CAIN AND SETSU.

The Heel siblings are born! ☆
Kyah~! A brother and sister who're wild and outside the limits! You look alike, and SO cool!
SETSU, SETSU.
Oh!
...
YES?
...
Y...
YES ?!

IF YOU LEAVE YOUR BROTHER ALONE, HE'LL CAUSE LOTS OF PROBLEMS...
...
...
...SO YOU TAKE CARE OF HIM.
UH ...
OKAY ...
OH...
I HEARD THAT I WAS GOING TO PLAY CAIN HEEL'S YOUNGER SISTER...
...SO I WAS WONDERING WHAT I'D HAVE TO DO...
But what a letdown...

I'M JUST HIS TEMPORARY MANAGER...
IF YOU LEAVE MR. TSURUGA ALONE, HE'LL HAVE PROBLEMS AT MEAL TIMES FOR SURE.
WHAT THE HELL. HOW COULD YOU?
IF YOU'RE REFER-RING TO MY EATING, I'LL BE FINE.
I'LL EAT WHEN I'M HUNGRY.
I CAN'T TRUST YOU!

End of Act 154

Skip·Beat!
Act 155: Violence Mission, Phase 3

WHAT THE HELL.
HOW COULD YOU?

IF YOU'RE REFERRING TO MY EATING, I'LL BE FINE.
I'LL EAT WHEN I'M HUNGRY.
What?
I CAN'T TRUST YOU!

Perfect health

MR. TSURUGA CAN'T TELL WHEN HE'S HUNGRY!
LOTS OF RESTAURANTS DELIVER TO THE HOTEL...
...SO CAIN HEEL CAN EAT WITHOUT HAVING PEOPLE WATCH HIM.
So you don't need to worry.
Huh?
AS CAIN HEEL?!
NO...
CAIN HEEL! HE SEEMS TO CARE ABOUT HIS HEALTH EVEN LESS THAN MR. TSURUGA.
His meals are alcohol.
With cigarettes for dessert.
Something like this.
WILL HE EAT PROPERLY AT ALL?!
I DON'T THINK HE WILL!
I trust him less than Mr. Tsuruga!
DON'T WORRY, PRESIDENT.

Hmm ?
I'LL...
...TAKE CARE OF MY BROTHER!
MS. MO-GAMI ...
Hey...
YEAH, YEAH.
I see, I see.
YOU REALLY CARE ABOUT YOUR BROTHER.
THEN ...
... HERE.
THIS.
Is for you.
HUH ?
tmp
THE HOTEL KEY TO THE ROOM CAIN HEEL WILL BE STAYING IN WHILE HE'S IN JAPAN.

YOU LIVE THERE...

...TO-GETHER...

...WITH YOUR BROTHER, ALL RIGHT?

WHAT ?!
Kyuubei
Kyuubei
Wel-come.
A table for four?
Blah
Blah

SORRY...
...TO KEEP YOU WAITING, CHIORI...
...WHEN WE WERE TALKING.
NO...
...I'M ALL RIGHT.
UM.
SO, WE WERE TALKING ABOUT THAT VARIETY SHOW.
That President Takarada forced on you today.
YES... I'M SORRY, I COULDN'T DEAL WITH PRESIDENT TAKARADA ALONE...
...SO I CALLED YOU TO HELP.
COME ON, THAT'S MY JOB AS YOUR MANA-GER.
I'M HERE TO PROTECT YOU.
...
YES.
YOU'RE AN ACTRESS...
...SO THERE'S NO NEED FOR YOU TO APPEAR IN A VARIETY SHOW AND HAVE PEOPLE LAUGH AT YOU.
Your image will be ruined.
ABOUT...
...THAT...

I'M...
...THINKING...
...ABOUT...
...ACCEPTING IT...
...AFTER ALL.
WHAT?!
WH-WHY?!
CHIORI, YOU WERE COMPLAINING ABOUT IT SO MUCH...
I'M SORRY...
Um...
SO...
...I FELT I SHOULD APOLOGIZE TO YOU FIRST...
For changing my mind like this...
NO...
YOU DON'T NEED TO APOLOGIZE...
DID HE SAY SOMETHING TO YOU AFTER THAT?!
AFTER I LEFT HIS OFFICE.
When I was shut out for three minutes.
chak
?!
Well... um...
UH...
BUT...
PRESIDENT TAKARADA ACCEPTED YOUR DECISION TO DECLINE.
...WHY?
HE SAID AGENCIES HAVE DIFFERENT POLICIES, AND THERE MIGHT BE SCHEDULING CONFLICTS...
HE ASKED ME AGAIN WHY I WANTED...
...TO BE A LOVE ME MEMBER.

...
AH...

TO GET BACK MY LOVE FOR ACTING...

...LIKE WHEN I WAS A CHILD...

MS. YOSHIMOTO.

Y-YES...

chuckle

UH...

I'M SORRY...

I couldn't help it...

A manager for 5 years.

An actress for 15 years.

...I THINK I SHOULD GO WITH PRESIDENT TAKARADA'S ...
... "DRASTIC MEASURES."
I...
...KNOW WHAT KIND OF ACTRESS I'D LIKE TO BE...
IT'S ...
...A HIGH-RISK GAMBLE...
...BUT I'M...
...DOING THIS...
...SO I CAN BECOME AN ACTRESS...
?
TO GET CLOSE TO THAT IDEAL...
... WHO ...
...CAN LOVE ALL THE CORNERS OF HER SOUL...

SO...
...WILL YOU HELP ME?
...AS YOUR MANAGER ...
OF COURSE ...
THAT'S MY JOB...
SECTIO

HOW ABOUT...
...DOING SOMETHING...
...THAT TAKES SOME GUTS?
YOU STOP ACTING...
...UNTIL YOU SIMPLY CAN'T RESIST...
...THE URGE...
...TO ACT.
YOU STOP...

...BEING AN ACTRESS FOR A WHILE.

SETSUKA.

YES...

...CAIN...

YOUR BROTHER IS APPALLED...

...BY THIS SITUA-TION.

One bed

THE PRESIDENT PLANS TO ENJOY HIMSELF WHILE TESTING MY RESOLVE...

I trust your resolve...

...But don't GO over-Board.

THAT'S WHAT HE MUST BE SAYING.

I-I'M SO SORRY...

IT'S ALL BECAUSE I WENT ALONG WITH THE PRESIDENT'S SWEET TALK...

NO... WELL IT'S NOT **JUST** YOUR FAULT.

THE PRESIDENT **IS** OVER-PROTECTIVE OF ME, AFTER ALL.

I DID PROVE THAT I COULD FOOL SOMEONE EVEN AFTER THEY FIGURED OUT IT WAS ME...

YOU NEED TO BE EXTRA CAUTIOUS.

YOU NEVER KNOW WHAT SORT OF DISASTER WILL HIT.

That's something someone you know says all the time.

grin

THAT GIRL...

... WARDS OFF EVIL.

...BUT I WOULDN'T HAVE BEEN THAT SURPRISED, AND I WOULD'VE KEPT MY GUARD UP...
...IF SHE HADN'T BEEN THE ONE WHO SHOWED UP.
Uh.
I know, Cain.

How about we get another room?
Great idea
I heard that the Room Rates are reasonable here.

I'll borrow money from the President to pay for my room—
THAT'S NOT POSSIBLE, SETSUKA.
I KNOW... I'LL BE SO SADDLED WITH DEBT...
She's still paying back her high school and acting school tuition fees. →
But you don't have to be so blunt...
NO... THAT'S NOT WHAT I MEAN.

AND SHE DOES HER JOB REALLY WELL...
SHEESH.
HE REAAAALLY DOESN'T TRUST ME...
No... he's toying with me...
WELL, I WAS IN DANGER DURING THE DISASTER DRILL...

SETSUKA HEEL.
TELL ME WHAT SORT OF PERSON YOU ARE.
OKAY.
ONE. SHE LOVES HER BROTHER.
TWO. SHE LOVES HER BROTHER.
THREE. SHE LOVES HER BROTHER.
FOUR. SHE LOVES HER BROTHER.
SHE ABSOLUTELY LOVES HER BROTHER. ♡
SHE'S GOT A BROTHER COMPLEX.
EXACTLY.
IT'S A SIMPLE SETUP...
THIS IS A TORTURE.
...THAT YOU CAN'T FORGET.
WOULD THAT SORT OF SISTER ...
...STAY IN A DIFFERENT ROOM FROM HER BROTHER?
...
NO... CAIN...

SHE WOULD ACTUALLY TRY TO SLEEP IN THE SAME BED AS HIM...

Ah... That's why there's only one bed...

U... UH...
I'LL SLEEP ON THE FLOOR ...
...IN A SLEEPING BAG...
I CAN'T MAKE A GIRL DO THAT—
Oh!
NO!

I WON'T LET MY BROTHER SLEEP ON THE FLOOR—
HOW ABOUT WE SLEEP TOGETHER ?

WHAT?

YOU CAN...
...SLEEP IN MY ARMS...

...
UH ...

ding don——g

WE...

...SINCERELY APOLOGIZE FOR OUR MISTAKE!

NO... IT'S ALL RIGHT.
Really.
YOU JUST GAVE US THE KEY TO THE WRONG ROOM.
I feel so relieved ...
THESE ARE COUPONS YOU CAN USE IN SHOPS NEAR THE HOTEL.
PLEASE TAKE THEM.
Really ?!
...

AH.
You don't need to do this.
We have two beds.
I...
...WAS SO CLOSE...

...TO GETTING HER...
...TO SAY...
..."I CAN'T DO THAT"...
IF SHE'D SAID SOME-THING LIKE THAT...

N-No... thanks...
I've never even dated!
How shameless!
I will not sleep in the same bed with a man!
...SHE'D...

...HAVE GOTTEN ANGRY...
THEN...
...I COULD'VE SAID THINGS TO HURT HER AND THEN SENT HER HOME.
"YOU LACK THE ACTOR'S SPIRIT."
"YOU...

... DON'T DE-SERVE TO BE MY PART-NER."

IF I...

fssh

...CAN CONTROL MYSELF...

sigh

...THERE WON'T BE ANY PROBLEMS...
I MEAN... I SHOULD GET AHOLD OF MYSELF...
I'M OLDER THAN SHE IS, AND I'VE BEEN ACTING LONGER THAN SHE HAS.
BUT...
...JUST THE TWO OF US...
...LIVING HERE...
...FOR WHO KNOWS HOW LONG...

...MAKES ME WORRY ABOUT THINGS...
...SO I WANTED TO HURT HER TO KEEP HER AWAY.

HOW PATHETIC...
I...
...WAS GOING TO HURT HER WITH WORDS THAT I DON'T EVEN MEAN.
I'M THE ONE WHO NEEDS...

...TO IMPROVE MY PROFES-SIONALISM AND ACTOR'S SPIRIT...
...SO I DON'T WAVER...
...NO MATTER WHAT HAPPENS.
AH...
WAH!
Ah!
tumble
tumble
SHEESH.
LOOK.
I SAID WE DIDN'T NEED ALL THIS STUFF.
Mister!

THEY FORCED ALL THIS ON ME.

In a way...

...this is...

...divine mischief.

A disaster.
hurry
scurry
She's not used to wearing this kind of thing, so she's not paying attention.
rustle
rustle
rustle
rustle
WOW...

THEY REALLY GAVE ME A LOT OF STUFF...

Coupons and all these hotel goodies.

AND THIS TEA THAT ISN'T EVEN FROM THE HOTEL.

Did they go out and buy this? I feel sorry for them...

THOSE POOR GUYS...

BOTH OF THEM WERE SO PALE...

THEY LOOKED REALLY FRIGHT-ENED...

...really scared.

THEY MUST'VE BEEN TERRI-FIED...

...OF MY "BIG BROTHER"...

Peek

HMM?

...
CAI-
GRAB

End of Act 155

Skip·Beat!
Act 156: Violence Mission, Phase 3.5

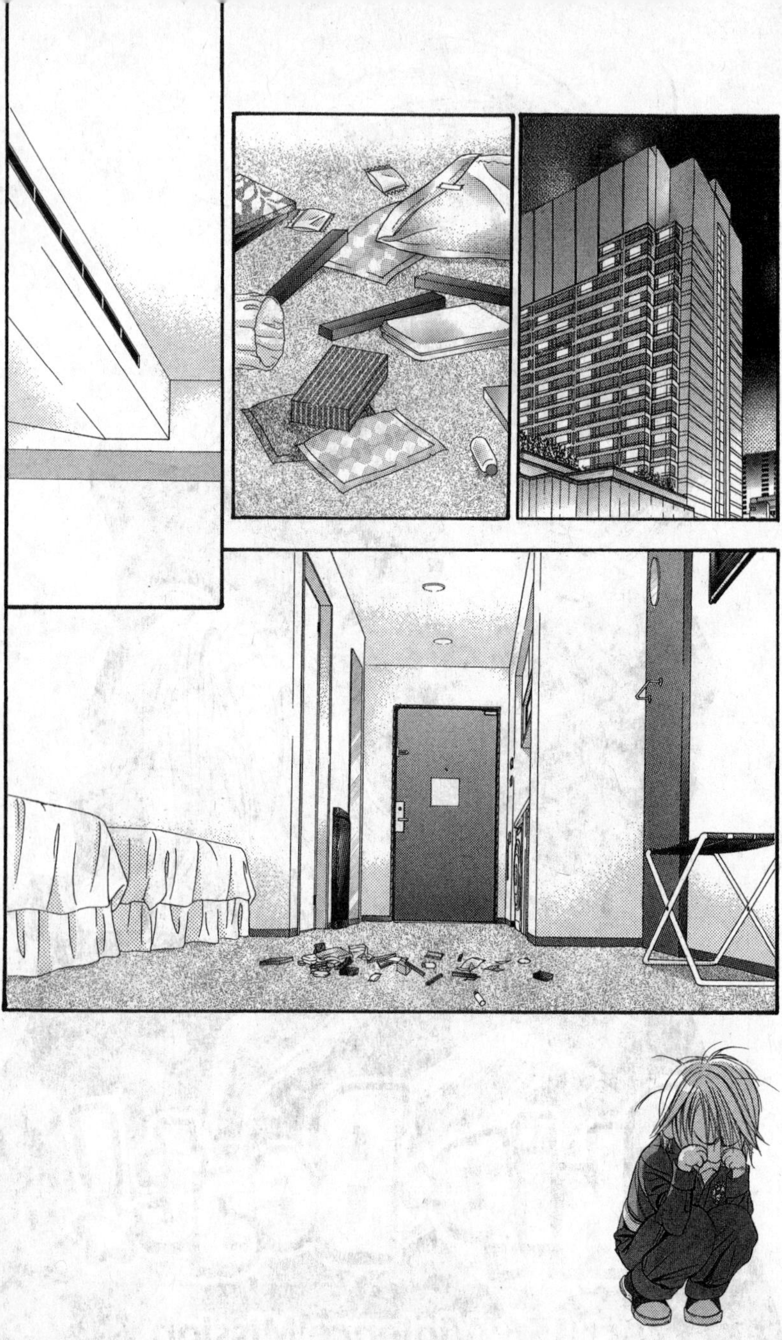

TRIP

CAIN...?

WHERE'RE YOU GOING ?!
STOMP
STOMP
STOMP
STOMP
clang
clang
TROMP

TROMP
TROMP
TROMP
MR. TSURUGA ?!

WHAT? WHAT'S GOING ON?!
WHY'RE YOU DOING THIS SO SUDDENLY ?!
I THOUGHT HIS MOOD CHANGED...
MR. TSURUGA!
...BACK THERE...

MOOD?
...
BUT...
...MY HEART...
...JUMPED...
...FOR A MOMENT.
HE DIDN'T LOOK LIKE HE WAS ABOUT TO KILL SOMEONE ...
HIS EYES WERE...
...SHIN- ING...
...WITH A STRANGE LIGHT.

MAYBE...
...MAYBE...
...HE'S ALREADY...
...CAIN?
MR. TSURUGA...

!
Oh!
She looks so awkward.
☆The Heel Siblings☆
☆Outlaws
☆Low-key
......
......
......
SHAKE
SHAKE
DRAG
DRAG
DRAG
TROMP
STOMP
STOMP
Calm
......

The Heel Siblings
Outlaws
Low-key
This isn't fair...
.....
Setsuka
..
..

TMP

Blah
Blah
MY FEET ...
... HURT ...
What's with that couple in black?
Are they dangerous or something?

YOU'RE WALKING ...
...TOO FAST...

Cafe Liana

stare

SILENCE

.....

Oh!

WHAT?!

WHY'D I RE-MEMBER THAT NOW?!

Why?

M-MAYBE ...

SHUP

NO GOOD.

He wants a retake.

tmp tmp

HUH ?!

DID MR. TSURUGA USE HIS TELEPATHIC ABILITIES TO SEND ME THAT MESSAGE?!
HE WASN'T REACTING TO BAD ACT-ING?!
...
Sigh
JOLT
HE'S SIGH-ING?!
SO MY ACTING WASN'T GOOD?!
TH-THUMP
Why not, why not?!
I was low-key.
I looked like an outsider.
I held his hand cuz I love my brother!
WHEN I COULD HAVE USED WORDS TO STOP HIM!
WHAT'S WRONG WITH MY ACTING?!
My brother!
SORRY...
THE STORE'S ABOUT TO CLOSE...
... SO ...

...I WAS IN A HURRY...
HMM?
WE'RE CONTIN-UING?
SO I DON'T NEED TO COR-RECT MY ACTING...
SO MAYBE I BARELY MANAGED TO PASS?
... THE STORE?
WHERE...
...ARE WE GOING?
JUST FOLLOW ME.
LET'S GO...

?
SETSU.
THIS WAY.
UH.

Darn.
I'M LOOKING AROUND TOO MUCH...
SORRY.
tmp
tmp
I'M OBSESSED WITH MY BROTHER, YET I TOOK MY EYES OFF HIM. HOW COULD I?!
Ah... Look.
It looks like the outside (Ren) is appalled.
Inside (Cain's soul)
Sigh
tmp
tmp
ARGH!
He sigh~ed! Agai~n!
The sighs of a retake
I'VE FAILED! I'VE FAILED THIS TIME FOR SURE!
Oh no~!
WHEN I'D JUST BARELY PASSED THE FIRST TIME!
He'll fire me for failing as Mr. Tsuruga's buddy~!
SETSU.

HURRY.
THE STORE WILL CLOSE.
...
OH?
tmp
tmp
HE'S...
...CONTIN-UING...
Jeanne d'Arc
JEANNE D'ARC?
ISN'T THIS THE BRAND MARIA LOVES?

GOOD EVENING.
tmp tmp tmp
?
?
SETSU.
YEAH?
YOU...
...DON'T HAVE A LOT TO WEAR, DO YOU?
!
UH...
HE'S RIGHT...
I...
...BROUGHT THESE FOR YOUR FITTING TODAY.
I'LL PACK THEM AS YOUR OTHER OUTFITS, SO WEAR THEM TOO.
Sorry! couldn't bring more.
Uh.
NO NO.
It's all right.
THANK YOU SO MUCH.
I JUST HAVE WHAT MS. JELLY THE MAGICAL MUSE GAVE ME...

I HAVE... THREE OR FOUR...
FIG-URES...
THIS IDEA MUST'VE COME UP AT THE LAST MOMENT...
The idea of Setsuka...
ALL RIGHT.
I'LL GET THEM FOR YOU.
CHOOSE SOME THINGS THAT YOU LIKE.
WHA...?!
Oh!
N-NO, I CAN'T LET MR. TSURUGA BUY ME CLOTHES!
No way! I can't have him do that!
I'LL BUY THEM MY-SELF!
IT'S ALL-
No...
HOLD IT!
Shut your mouth now!
MY BROTHER.
THE BROTHER I LOVE IS SAYING HE'LL BUY ME CLOTHES!

I'LL FAIL AS SETSUKA IF I'M MODEST AND REFUSE HIS OFFER!
He'll mercilessly sigh a "no"!
I should... happily go along with his offer!
...
"IT'S ALL"?
Heh
grin

YOU...
...SURE?
IF YOU'RE GONNA BUY ME CLOTHES...
...I'M...
...GONNA...
...GET LOOOOOTS.
chuckle chuckle
OKAY?
Heh.

SURE.
GET WHAT-EVER...
...YOU WANT.

clang
...
THAT IS THE FIRST TIME...
clang
clang
...HE'S SMILED AT ME...
...AFTER COM-PLETELY BECOMING...
...CAIN HEEL...
DOES THAT MEAN...
...WHAT I JUST SAID...

...WAS OKAY FOR SETSUKA?
grin
...
SMI~LE
grin grin
YAAAY!
WAS IT?
whisper whisper
stare stare
Oh!
!
NNN.
STOIC
ANY-WAY...
...THANKS TO WHAT CAIN JUST SAID, I THINK I UNDERSTAND US A LITTLE BETTER NOW...
I MAY LOVE MY BROTHER TOO MUCH, BUT CAIN...

...LOVES HIS SISTER WAY TOO MUCH TOO!
YOU'RE WEARING WORN-OUT SHOES...
Her brother's shoes
peeling
this side too
HE SAID!
"GET WHATEVER YOU WANT." HE DOTES ON HIS SISTER!
Only a grandpa or grandma who loves their grandchild too much would say that!
BECAUSE YOU DOTE ON HER...
...YOUR SISTER LOVES YOU SO MUCH. IT'S NO LONGER JUST EXTREME, IT'S SICK!
IT MUST'VE BEEN CAUSED BY AN INFINITE FEEDBACK LOOP...
What a scary world it is...
THE BROTHER SHE LOVES IS COLD TO OTHER PEOPLE, BUT REALLY NICE TO HER AND DOTES ON HER.
THE SISTER CLINGS TO HER BROTHER AND ACTS LIKE A BABY.
THE BROTHER FINDS THAT SISTER LOVABLE AND DOTES ON HER EVEN MORE.
AND THE SISTER CLINGS TO HER BROTHER EVEN TIGHTER...

Oh!
AH...
...
I SEE...
I get it...
I SHOULD'VE ...
...EX-PRESSED MY FEELINGS MORE SINCE I...
... BEHAVE LIKE A BABY.
I SHOULD'VE GOTTEN ANGRY...
...OR POUTED.
I SHOULD'VE ...
...HURLED MY FEELINGS ...

...AT MY BROTHER...

COMPARED...
GLOOM
...TO MR. TSURUGA, MY UNDERSTANDING OF MY ROLE IS TOO SUPERFICIAL...
Truthfully, I had no idea what a sister who loves her brother too much would do...
MAYBE I HAVEN'T MATURED AT ALL SINCE I STARTED ACTING IN DARK MOON...
...

...EVEN IF I'M BEING SELFISH.

THAT'S WHY HE SIGHED A "NO."

IF I'D...

...ACTED RIGHT BACK THERE...

...HOW WOULD MR. TSURUGA...

...HAVE RESPONDED?

End of Act 156

A Mysterious Valentine's Incident Part 2 *The Kyoko Mogami chapter*

GOOD.
I HAD THE AGENCY CHANGE MY CELL PHONE NUMBER.
And I turned caller ID off, so the Beagle can't sniff out my radio waves!
NOW I WON'T RECEIVE ANY HARASSING CALLS FROM THE BEAGLE.
snap
brrring
HMM?
flipp
No Caller ID
brrrring
...
IS IT MR. SAWARA?
Or...
bip
Hmph.
Your resistance is useless.
Too bad, but no matter what you do, you can't get away from me—
NOOOOOOOOOOOOO!
Save me, monster hunter!
DASH DASH DASH DASH
?!
You call-ing ME a mon-ster?!
Hey, don't run away! Where'd you go?!
SHO, IF YOU WANT KYOKO TO DEAL WITH YOU, JUST CALL HER. DON'T PLAY TRICKS ON HER.
I understand that she'll hang up as soon as she knows it's you, but...
Of course she'd run away if you make a weird phone call like that!
U-Um...
A voice changer
MS. ASAMI... PLEASE SCOLD SHO FOR HACKING YOUR CELL PHONE AGAIN...
Sho got Kyoko's number from Ms. Haruki's cell phone. Her password is her birthday, so Sho easily hacked it.

TRAFFIC SAFETY

Skip-Beat! End Notes

Everyone knows how to be a fan, but sometimes cool things from other cultures need a little help crossing the language barrier.

Page 199, panel 1: Natsuko, likes people
A pun on its name. *Hitonatsukkoi* means "likes people."

Page 236, panel 4: Hachi statue
This statue commemorates a dog that waited every day at the station for its master to get home, even after the master passed away. It is a popular place to meet.

Skip·Beat!

Skip·Beat!

Volume 27

CONTENTS

I FELT...
...NOT SO LONG AGO...
...THIS SAME KIND OF EMOTION ...

Skip·Beat!
Act 157: Violence Mission, Phase 4

Sizzle

Puff

CAIN.

YOU KNOW WHAT YOU WANT?
IT'S KIND OF EXPENSIVE.
WHICH ONE?
I DON'T CARE.

IT'S OUR MONTHLY SPECIAL...
Baphomet (a devil)
¥700,000 for the complete set
...

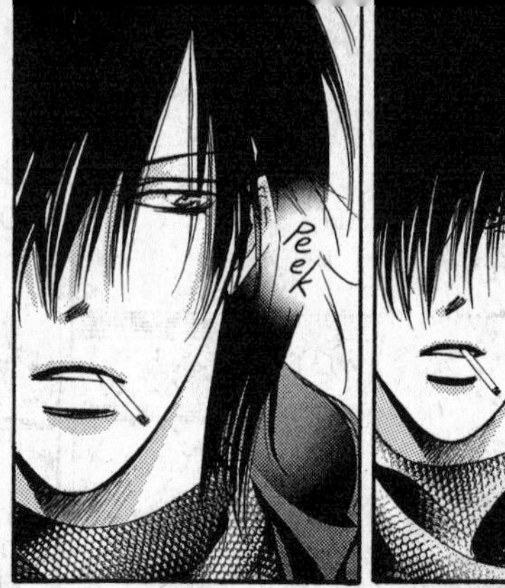
Peek

SETSU.

YES?

YOU REALLY WANT THIS?

oh!

!

She's obviously expecting some-thing.
STARE

I do.

nod

REALLY.

...
So expressive, it's like she's speaking.
th-thump th-thump
th-thump th-thump

WE'LL TAKE IT, THEN.

blasé

Take it off the rack.

Poit

JOLT

!

TH-THANK YOU SO MUCH!!

NOOOOOOOO!
GRAB
WHAT?
A... ARE YOU SURE?
ABOUT WHAT?
IT'S REALLY EXPEN-SIVE.
...
DON'T WORRY.
THE DESIGN'S VERY ORIGINAL ...
DON'T WORRY.
YOU LOOK GOOD IN ANY-THING.
Cuz you're cute.
I CAN AF-FORD IT.
YOU'RE NOT HESITATING EVEN A LITTLE?! THERE'RE FIVE ZEROS ON THE PRICE TAG!
TH...
YOU STUPID BROTHER!
GRRR
HOW MUCH DO YOU DOTE ON YOUR SISTER?!

...
WHAT'S WRONG?
YOU WANT THIS, DON'T YOU?
NO, I DON'T WANT SOMETHING CREEPY LIKE THAT.
CATS AND DOGS DON'T GROW UP TO BE SMART IF YOU JUST DOTE ON THEM!
You should discipline your family members!
POUT
THEN WHY'D YOU SAY YOU WANT THIS?
You're making no sense...
IT'S BE-CAUSE ...
I WANTED YOU TO SAY NO.
I WANTED YOU TO COAX AND CONVINCE ME THAT IT'S "TOO EXPENSIVE" AND "NOT PRACTICAL."
BUT YOU WENT ALONG WITH ME.
...I WANTED TO ANNOY YOU.

Are you going through a rebellious phase? How dare you?
IS THIS THE MOUTH THAT'S GIVING SUCH SASS?
GRAB
N...
NO. THAT'S MY CHEEK AND MY MOUTH IS H-
IS THIS THE MOUTH THAT'S GIVING SUCH SASS?
STRETCH
Not your ears or your nose.
It's your mouth.
This is your mouth.
Right?
.....
.....

IT'S... IT'S THE REIGN OF TERROR!
I...I'M SORRY ...
This is my mouth... yes. You're right. Sort of...
No.
YOUR SISTER CAN'T LOVE A BROTHER LIKE THIS!
WELL... WE'VE FOOLED AROUND ENOUGH.
Wha?
HE WAS FOOLING AROUND ?!
HERE, SETSU ...
And my cheek really, really hurts!
tingle
I DIDN'T GET IT!
I was sure he was just threatening me.
TOSS
?!
TRY ...
...THAT ON.
...

A PAIR OF PANTS ...
tmp
yank
bend
bend
pat
pat
YUP.

ka chak
IT'S EASY TO MOVE AROUND IN THIS.
tmp
I'M READY ...
... CAIN.
AH.
He made her wear this too.
WHAT DO YOU THINK?
I LIKE IT.
FEELS GOOD.
IT'S COMFY AND I CAN MOVE AROUND IN THIS.
I...
...THOUGHT THE TIGHT, SUPER-SHORT SKIRT WAS HARD TO MOVE IN.
I WAS WEARING SHORTS UNDER-NEATH TO HIDE MY UNDER-WEAR...
...BUT STILL ...

MAYBE...
...MR. TSURUGA NOTICED?
THANKS...
...CAIN.
I...
...ACTUALLY...
...WANTED SOMETHING LIKE THIS...
KNOWING YOU...
...I FIGURED YOU'D SAY THAT...
YEAH...
...SO I ALREADY BOUGHT TEN MORE.
WHAM
EXCUSE US FOR MAKING YOU WAIT.
?!
¥18,000 a pair

YOU'RE ACTING LIKE A REAL WASTREL.

YOU SHOULD BE MORE CAREFUL ABOUT HOW YOU SPEND YOUR MONEY.
Why'd you buy ten identical pairs of pants?!
YOU'RE WASTING TOO MUCH MONEY!
I CAN DO WHATEVER I WANT WITH THE MONEY I EARNED.
OF COURSE YOU CAN.

I WOULDN'T BE COMPLAINING IF YOU WERE USING YOUR MONEY FOR **YOURSELF**.

I'M COMPLAINING CUZ YOU KEEP WASTING YOUR MONEY ON **ME**!

I CAN'T HELP IT.

IT'S MORE FUN SPENDING MONEY ON YOU THAN ON MYSELF.

GNH
B...
BUT...
SO, WHAT?
ARE YOU...
...GONNA TAKE AWAY THE ONE PLEASURE...
...BESIDES ACTING...
...THAT...
...I HAVE?

WH...
You look like an abandoned puppy!
Sad eyes
Stare
Whine
Cain
WHAT KIND OF FACE IS THAT?!
Stop! Stop!
IT FEELS LIKE I'M BULLY-ING YOU!
UGH ...
GUILT
Sting
Sting
W...
WELL ...
Uh
Um
I DIDN'T TELL YOU TO COM-PLETELY STOP DOTING ON ME.
I JUST DON'T WANT YOU TO GO OVER-BOARD.
TODAY ...

I'M COMPLAINING CUZ YOU BOUGHT TEN PAIRS WHEN TWO WOULD'VE BEEN ENOUGH.
I...
...I'M...
... ALWAYS HAPPY ...
...WHEN YOU BUY ME SOME-THING...
...SO PLEASE.
JUST KEEP TWO PAIRS...

...SO I CAN THANK YOU HONESTLY FOR THEM...
...AND RETURN THE REST TO THE STORE...
...
THREE PAIRS.
!
NO.
TWO'S ENOUGH.
...
Three pairs...
mumble
There's more now.
whine whine whine
Cain
Cainmaru
Caingo
!

And she lost.
tmp
tmp
...
...
...

WASN'T I SUPPOSED TO DO THAT TO HIM?
IT'S ...
...A LITTLE DIFFERENT FROM THE BROTHER I'D IMAGINED...

WHAT SORT OF SIBLING RELATION-SHIP IS THIS...?
.....
WHAT IS THIS ...?
WHY...
...IS THE YOUNGER SISTER COAXING AND DISCIPLINING THE BIG BROTHER WHO'S SO UNREASON-ABLE?

I THOUGHT CAIN...
...would be more...
...COOL AND BRUSQUE, AND ONLY NICE TO HIS SISTER...
A GROWN-UP WHO'S UNDER-STANDING, LIKE A GUARDIAN.

BUT HE SHOWS NO MERCY.

IS THIS THE MOUTH THAT'S GIVING SUCH SASS?
Are you going through a rebellious phase? How dare you?
GRAB
N...
NO. THAT'S MY CHEEK AND MY MOUTH IS H--
IS THIS THE MOUTH THAT'S GIVING SUCH SASS?
With a vengeance.

HE DOESN'T PLAN AHEAD.

I CAN AFFORD IT.
YOU'RE NOT HESITATING EVEN A LITTLE?! THERE'RE FIVE ZEROS ON THE PRICE TAG!
TH...
...SO I ALREADY BOUGHT TEN MORE.
WHAM
EXCUSE US FOR MAKING YOU WAIT.
?!
¥18,000 a pair

AND MOREOVER...

HE WHINES LIKE A BABY.

I CAN'T HELP...

...THINKING...

...WHEN HE ACTS LIKE A KID...

...THAT HE'S CUUUTE! DARN IIIIIT! SHALL I MAKE YOU ACT LIKE A BABY SOME MOOOORE?!
Rah~~!
The new Setsuka, just now born.
Has a foul mouth.
SOME-THING LIKE THAAAAAAAT!
Pa~nt pant pant
thump thump thump
SQUIRM SQUIRM
CAIN, WITH HIS LOOKS AND PHYSIQUE...
...ACTING LIKE A CHILD....

IT ISN'T FAIR AT AAAAALL!
OOH ...
I...
...
... WANT TO SEE MORE ...
...OF MR. TSURUGA REACT-ING AS CAIN...
...WHEN I'M SETSUKA.
YES, LOTS OF IT!

I'VE...
...FELT THIS EMOTION ...
AND...
...NOT LONG AGO.
THIS IS...

Clomp
Clomp
Clomp

Pat
!
Huh?
...
WEL-COME BACK.

DID YOU APOLOGIZE TO THE SALES CLERK?

NOOOOPE.
I DIDN'T APOLOGI-I-I-IZE.

CUZ WE DIDN'T DO ANYTHING WROOOOONG.

WHAT DO YOU THINK ABOUT A RESTAURANT THAT SERVES RICE THAT ISN'T COOKED RIGHT?

How could they? They duped us!

OF **COURSE** THE CUSTOMER HAS A RIGHT TO SNAP AND GET VIOLENT.

THE OWNER AND EMPLOYEES CAN'T COMPLAIN, EVEN IF THEY GET A COUPLE OF BROKEN TEETH.

chat chat

SOOOOOO.
WE'RE GONNA GO SOME-WHERE ELSE.
grin
grin
OUR TREAT, SO WHY DON'T YOU COME WITH US?
AND ...
...AFTER THAT WE'LL TAKE YOU SOME-WHERE FUN.

I...
... DON'T MIND ...
!
Really?! Woo woo! ♡
I WAS SURE AN EASY-LOOKING GIRL LIKE YOU WOULD SAY YES.
I love cute girls like that! ♡
Me too, me too.
I...

... DON'T MIND...
Hmm?
BUT...
...IF YOU WANNA PLAY WITH ME...
...YOU HAVE TO GET PERMISSION TO BORROW ME...
... FROM ...
!

...THE DARLING ...
...OVER THERE.
End of Act 157

Skip·Beat!
Act 158: Violence Mission, Phase 5
TORE

BROTHER
...

THESE
GUYS...

...WANNA
PLAY
WITH
ME.

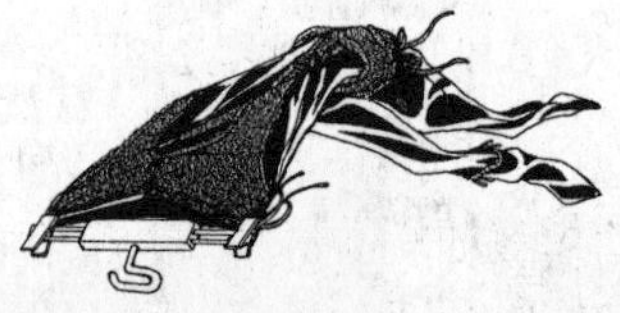

...MAY I?

BROTHER?
OH.
I THOUGHT "THE DARLING" WAS YOUR BOYFRIEND, BUT HE'S JUST YOUR BROTHER.
UGH.
A BOYFRIEND WOULD'VE BEEN EASIER TO NEGOTIATE WITH.
A LOT OF BOYFRIENDS LOVE TO LOAN OUT THEIR GIRLFRIENDS.
A 100% success rate.
BUT IF YOU'RE HER BROTHER, YOU WON'T ABANDON HER JUST CUZ YOU CARE MORE FOR YOURSELF THAN HER.
NO NO, IT'S THE SAME WITH SIBLINGS.
SINCE HUMAN BEINGS LOVE THEM-SELVES THE MOST.
RIGHT...
...BROTHER?

I'M WARNING YOU.
JUST LET US BORROW YOUR SISTER...
...FOR A LITTLE WHILE.
shf
...
SETSU.
LET'S GO.
!
!
YEEEES.
!
HE JUST IGNORED US.
Like Kei was an insect.
How could he?!
And I was trying to do this the nice way.
IT'S ALL RIGHT.
Hya hya hya

clench
NOW KAZU'S GOT AN EXCUSE TO GET VIOLENT.
crack crack
flip
DASH
SHWIP

freeze
!
?!
...

grin
Beeeeep beep.
OOPS.
KAZU'S SWITCH IS ON NOW.
HUH? WHAT? MAYBE THAT GUY'S GOOD AT FIGHTING?
OOH, SO HE DOESN'T JUST LOOK STRONG.
IF I CAN'T HAVE THE SISTER ...
... FOR ...
...THE BROTHER'LL DO JUST FINE...
shf

shk
...ME...
Ha
...TO PLAY WITH...
SHOOM
WHAM

!

HE DUCKED.

I'VE NEVER SEEN ANYONE DUCK KAZU'S LEFT HOOK!

So he really CAN fight.

NOOOO, HE MIGHT'VE JUST GOTTEN LUCKY.

CUZ LOOK. HE'S JUST...

... DODGING.

Ah.

MAYBE...

shuuu

...HE'S GOOD AT AVOIDING A PUNCH, BUT NOT SO GOOD AT THROWING ONE?

Setsu's soul
.....
MR. TSURUGA!

WH...
WHAT SHOULD I DO...?
What's going on? Scary!
A huge man in Black and a huge macho man.
Should we call the police?
IF THIS ENDS WITH SOMEONE GETTING HURT...
WON'T PEOPLE FIND OUT THAT MR. TSURUGA IS CAIN HEEL?!
Won't the police investigate him?!
NO, IF THAT HAPPENS ...
...THE MOVIE WILL BE RUINED!
EVEN IF PEOPLE DON'T FIND OUT RIGHT NOW...
...EVERYONE WILL BASH HIM FOR THIS...
...WHEN CAIN HEEL'S IDENTITY IS REVEALED AFTER THE MOVIE PREMIERES!
Maybe there's a hidden camera, and they're shooting a drama or something.
Whoa.
I'll re-cord it.
MR. TSURUGA'S A CELEBRITY.

IF HE HURTS A CIVILIAN EVEN ONCE...!
BUT...

...IF YOU WANNA PLAY WITH ME...
...YOU GET PERMISSION TO BORROW ME...
...FROM...

IF I HADN'T INSISTED ON STAYING IN MY ROLE...
...IF I HAD JUST SAID NO OR RAN AWAY...!
WHAM
WHY DON'T YOU PUNCH BACK?!
WHAM
YOU BASTARD.
KICK
DUCK
...
HE KEEPS MISSING ...
HE'S DUCKING AT THE LAST MINUTE.
ISN'T KAZU JUST WEARING HIMSELF OUT?
...
MAYBE... THAT'S THE POINT?

TO WEAR KAZU OUT AND THEN GET HIM IN ONE SHOT...
WHAMM

GLARE
!

YES...
I'LL TAKE MR. TSURUGA AWAY FROM THAT MACHO AND VIOLENT MAN...
...AND RUN AWAY AT THE SPEED OF LIGHT!
TH-THE BEST THING TO DO NOW IS TO RUN AWAY!
CALM DOWN, CALM DOWN, HEART!
th-thump th-thump th-thump th-thump
gulp
B-But.
What to do?
Panic Panic Panic Panic
CHAKUN
CHAK
CHAK
!
H...
HEEEEEEY!

...
twitch
YAH!
SWING
snap
THUD
...
CAIN, WATCH OUT BE-HIND YOU!
SKKKSHSH

WHAP
!
You coward!
HUH?!
GRAB GRAB
Being a worse human than Sho Fuwa...
...is embarrassing! Hopeless!
How dare you all attack one person! You guys are worse than Sho Fuwaaaaa!
...and just take your friends out to eat!
WAH!
You don't want that, so throw your weapons away...
Hey, let GO!
No way!

GET OUTTA MY WAY!
SWINNG
Move it!
...
WHAM
FWIP

GRAB
...
SWING
WHAMM

Con-
cussion
Waaaaaaah.
wah wah waah
K-
Kazu!
No~~!
shff—
No~~~
No...

Whooo...

End of Act 158

Skip·Beat!
Act 159: Violence Mission, Phase 5.5

I'M...
...GOING TO BE A COLD-BLOODED, HOMICIDAL FIEND IN A MOVIE.

EVEN AFTER THE MOVIE IS RELEASED...
...WE WON'T TELL PEOPLE...

...RIGHT AWAY THAT REN TSURUGA...
...PLAYED THE ROLE.

He's...

...like an arrow shot from the darkness.

The arrow flies with the wind, approaching its prey silently...

...and then pierces its target.

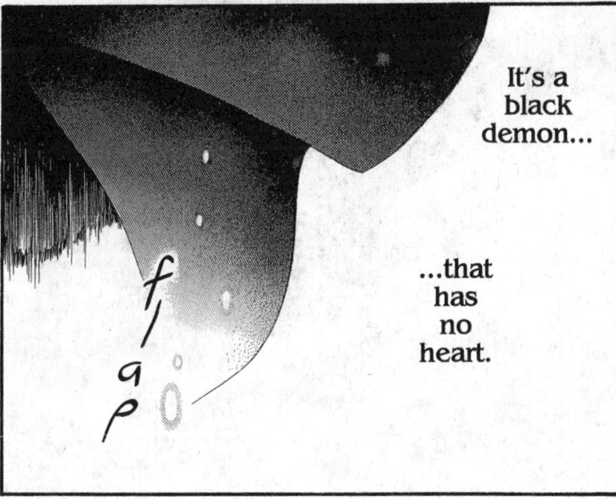

It's a black demon...
...that has no heart.
flap

DASH

B...
K-!!!!
K-!!!!
K-!!!!
Kyaah
Kyaah
WHP
WHP
NO...
BJ!

N...
DASHDASH
DASH
DASH
SHOOOM
SHOOOOM
SKKKKKKKSH
SHOOOM
SHOOM
SHOO
NOOOO!

R...
RUUUUUN! RUN FOR YOUR LIFE, SEAWEED HEAD!
Plea--se!
You're slow!
You're too slow! Faster!
Awa wa wa wa wa wah
WHAT'RE WE GONNA DO IF YOU GET KILLED?!

MR. TSURUGAAAA!
MR. TSURUGA WOULD NORMALLY THINK ABOUT WHAT WOULD HAPPEN IF HE HURTS THAT GUY...
...BUT HE'S BEEN COMPLETELY TAKEN OVER BY BJ!
WHAT SHOULD I DO?!
I GOTTA STOP HIM!

CAIN ...
MR. TSURUGA ...
...
NO!
D...

DON'T KILL HIIIIIIM!

KILLER!
SHKK

THUD
WHAM
GYAH!
shiver
!
THUD
...
...
...
...
D...
Peek
Peek
DID HE... KILL HIM?
th-thump th-thump th-thump
YES?
Gnh...
Wooooooooo
Oh?
Why's he holding the back of his head?
What happened?

What happened
SHOOM
G
!
whp
Ren didn't connect...
WHAM
...but the guy tripped...
SLAM
THUD
Gyah!
WHAM
...and fell down.
?
th-thump th-thump
tmp
tmp
MR. TSURUGA DIDN'T PUNCH HIM...
CUZ IN ORDER...
...TO GET PUNCHED IN THE BACK OF THE HEAD...
tmp
tmp
...SEAWEED HAIR WOULD'VE HAD TO FLIP VERTICALLY IN THE AIR...
And no way that wimp could've done that...

IN ANY CASE, I'M GLAD MR. TSURUGA STOPPED HIMSELF...
...
CAI-

...
MR....
TWITCH
grab
...TSU-RUGA?

fwip
!
th-thump

...MR. TSURUGA?
OR ...

WHO ...
...AM I?
THERE WAS A BLACK DEMON INSIDE ME NOW...
EXHAUSTED
YES.
Yes...
IT TOOK YOU OVER... COMPLETELY ...
From the top of your head to the tip of your toes...
I'D LIKE TO ASK YOU THAT!
Are you Mr. Tsuruga?! Or Cain Heel?! Which is it?!
...IS IT CAIN HEEL?
...
AM I...
... STILL ...
... POSSESSED BY HIM?
SETSU ...
...I
WHA?

grin

NO.

YOU'RE CAIN HEEL.

YOU'RE MY DEAR, CUTE, AND KLUTZY BIG BROTHER.

SO IT...

What do you mean, klutzy?

How dare you say that to your Brother.

This wasn't work, but you were about to kill him. You're too quick on the trigger.

I could call you hopeless, instead.

Just call me a klutz, then.

...

End of Act 159

Skip·Beat!
Act 160: Violence Mission, Phase 6

CAIN...

WHAT ...?

WHAT ARE THESE?

CAN'T YOU TELL? THEY'RE YOURS (ALL SHIRTS).

......
......

I RETURNED THE PANTS, SO YOU SHOULDN'T COMPLAIN.

Hmph!

Returning the pants doesn't make it better if you turned around and bought all these other clothes!
I made you return them so you wouldn't waste your money.
YOU JUST NEED TO WEAR ALL OF THEM ENOUGH SO THEY DON'T ROT IN THE CLOSET.
clink clank
IT'S UP TO YOU WHETHER I WASTED MONEY OR NOT.
IT SHOULDN'T BE DIFFICULT.
HE'S FIGHTING BACK! HE'S ON THE OFFENSIVE!
First he begged, and now he's being aggressive?!
ALL OF THEM ...
YOU SHOULD BE ABLE TO WEAR THEM ALL.

grin
CUZ YOU'RE A GIRL.
A skillful psycho-logical attack
!
W...
WELL YEEES.
Of course.
Heh heh heh
I only need 15 days to wear all of them at least once!
Female Pride
Leaning Tower of Pi
YOU LOVE CLOTHES, SO I FIGURED YOU'D SAY THAT.
Right?
I'M SURE YOU'D LOVE TO HAVE MORE THINGS...
...BUT MAKE DO WITH WHAT YOU HAVE NOW.
At least until this gig is done.
YOU LOVE DRESSING UP, SO YOU CAN DO IT.
...
...
Setsuka is a STYLISH, FASHION-ABLE Girl.
Emphasis
HE'S MAKING THINGS MORE AND MORE DIFFI-CULT!
tmp tmp
WELL, I'M...
...GOING TO TAKE A SHOWER...

ka chak
...SO PUT YOUR PRE-CIOUS CLOTHES IN THE CLOSET.
chak
I FEEL LIKE I'VE BEEN SWEET-TALKED INTO SUBMIS-SION!
HE ENDED UP BUYING MORE STUFF, AND THE TOTAL COST MUST BE WAY OVER THE TEN PAIRS OF PANTS!
I SHOULD'VE JUST ACTED HAPPY AND BROUGHT HOME THOSE PANTS!
I SHOULDN'T HAVE BEEN DUPED BY HIS CUTE WORDS AND ACTIONS.
He's a sly lion that pretends to be an innocent puppy.
grumble grumble
freeze
fold fold
Yes.
CUZ CAIN HEEL IS BASED ON MR. TSURUGA!

.....
TMP
MR. TSURUGA'S ...
... EXPRESSION...
... THEN ...
WAS IT...
...REALLY...
...AN ACT?
AFTER-WARDS, MR. TSURUGA SAID...
I'M A LITTLE WORRIED ...
THANKS, SETSU.

I WAS ABOUT TO DESTROY HALF THAT GUY'S FACE.
...
HE'S JOKING... RIGHT?
About this.
You can't crush someone's face so easily...
NO MATTER WHAT THE CIRCUM-STANCES...
...PEOPLE IN OUR BUSINESS GET INTO TROUBLE IF WE USE FORCE.
...
I MIGHT'VE ENDED UP TRASHING THE MOVIE ITSELF.
YES.
WHEN I CALMED DOWN, I SHIVERED WITH FEAR.
THANKS ...

...FOR STOPPING ME.
Heh
YOU'RE TELLING ME NOW?

shak
AS CAIN HEEL...
shak
THAT'S HOW I TOOK IT...

...BUT THINGS DON'T MAKE SENSE SOMEHOW...
CUZ...
...IF MR. TSURUGA WAS STILL ACTING AS CAIN HEEL...

IT'S MY DUTY TO TAKE CARE OF MY BROTHER.

"WHEN I CALMED DOWN, I SHIVERED WITH FEAR."

...HE SHOULDN'T...

...HAVE LOST HIMSELF SO COMPLETELY...

...AND LOOKED SO STUNNED.

AH.

SETSU, HOLD IT.

ALMOST FORGOT THIS.

Heave-ho.

He'd hung it up, so it wouldn't get dirty.

Setsu's clothes. Important

Now I remember. You weren't carrying it!

WHEN DID YOU HAVE THE TIME TO HANG IT, WHEN THE MACHO VIOLENT DUDE WAS ATTACKING YOU SO FIERCELY?!

Cain, you!

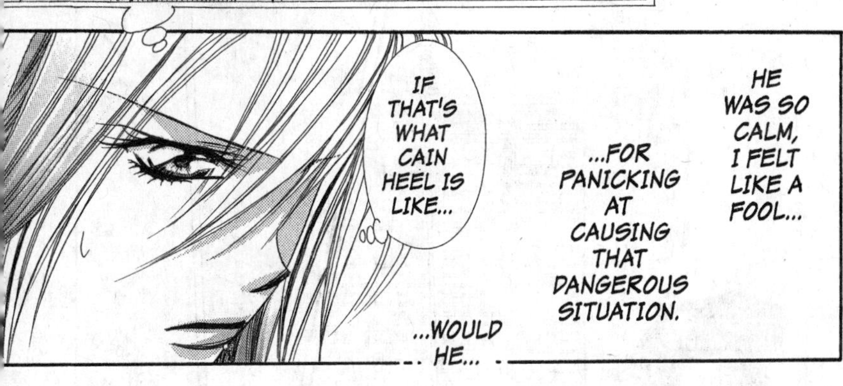

HE WAS SO CALM, I FELT LIKE A FOOL...
...FOR PANICKING AT CAUSING THAT DANGEROUS SITUATION.
IF THAT'S WHAT CAIN HEEL IS LIKE...
...WOULD HE...

...SO EASILY...

...BEHAVE IN A WAY...

...THAT MADE EVEN HIS SISTER...

...FEEL UNEASY?

...WAS ACTUALLY...
kssh
ksssh
ksssh

kssh

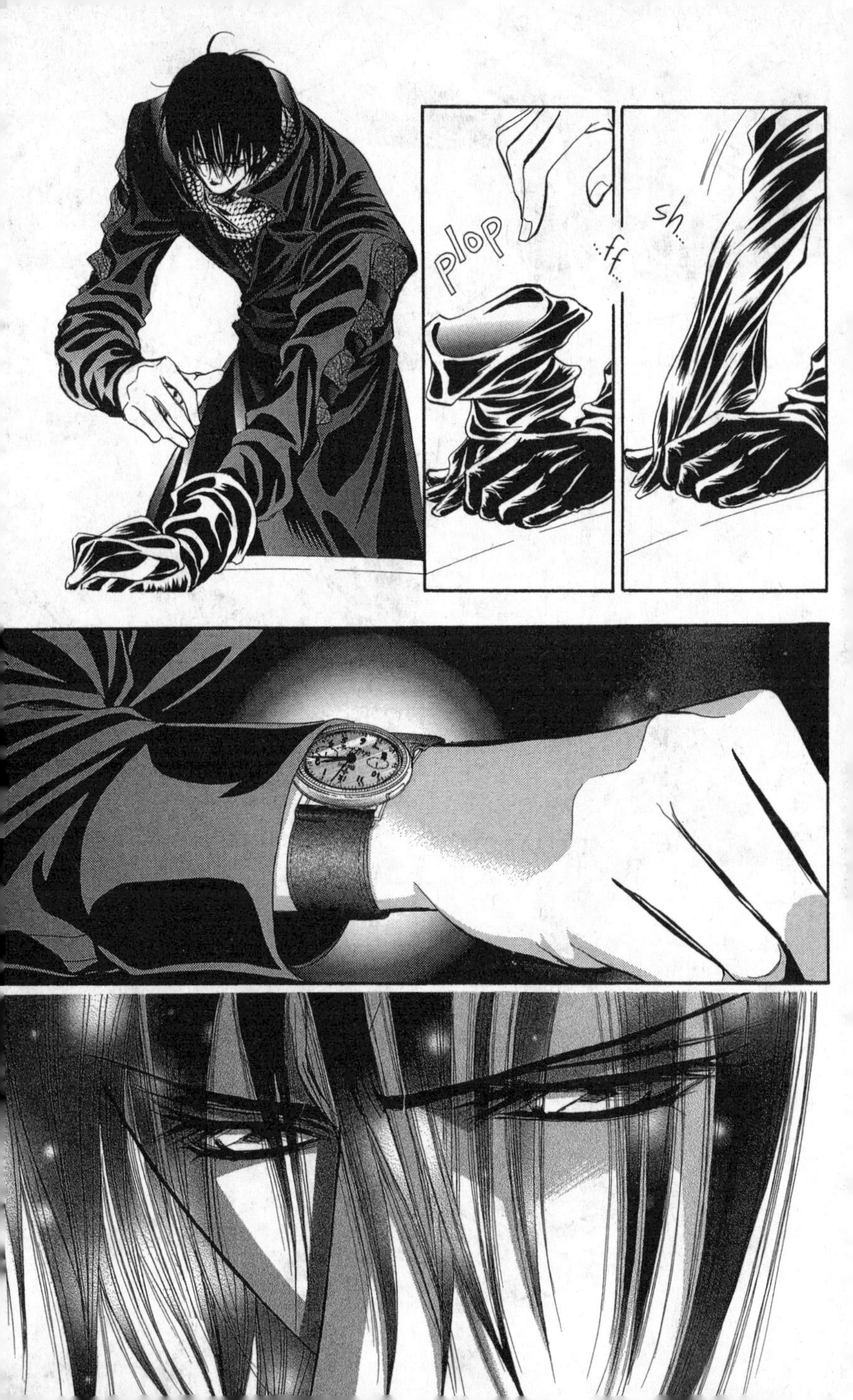

plop
sh...
...ff...

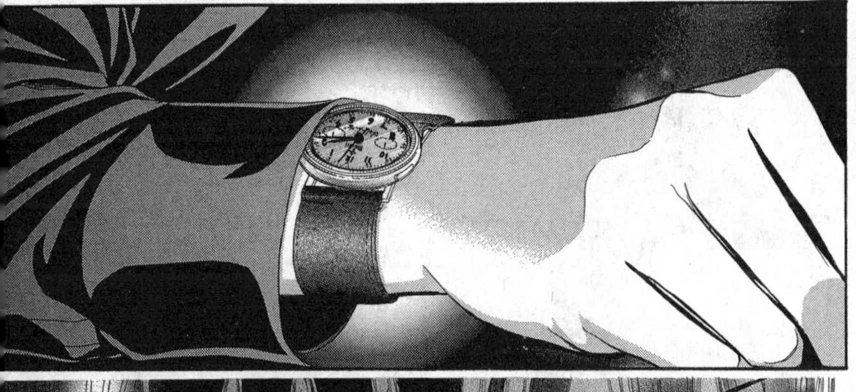

grab
kssh

kssh

...

kssh

ISN'T...

...HE TAKING...

...AN AWFULLY LONG TIME?

I THOUGHT MEN TAKE SHORT BATHS...

But it's been 40 minutes...

LIKE HE SOAKS IN THE BATHTUB WITH ROSE PETALS...
She thinks like the General public
glom
kssh
BUT... I DON'T THINK HE'S RELAXING IN THE BATH-TUB.

SHOTARO TOOK 15 MINUTES IN THE MORNING, AND 20 MINUTES AT NIGHT...

OR IS IT JUST BECAUSE IT'S MR. TSURUGA?

Maybe he takes showers differently than the General public?

Oh!

M-MAYBE ...

HE FELL ASLEEEEEEP?!
No! What're you doing?!
Like this
...here...
What a bother... I'll sleep...
ZZZZ
Using the towel as a blanket
kssh
YOU'LL CATCH A COOOOOLD!
Cain!
CHAKA

kssh
WHAT IS IT...?
chk
grin

YOU WANNA JOIN ME?

smile
shaa
TAKE YOUR TIME.
SURE.
IF I WASN'T COOKING ...
...I'd Love TO!♡
SORRY, I THOUGHT YOU MIGHT'VE FALLEN ASLEEP AND...
...GOT A LITTLE TOO WOR-RIED.

Chak
.....
.....

NOOOOOOOOOOOO
OOOOOOOOOOOO

I DIDN'T MEAN TO SEE HIM!
NO!
I HARDLY SAW ANYTHING! NO! I ONLY SAW HIS FACE! HIS FAAAAACE!
OH!
KYAAAAAAAAAAAAAAAAAAAH
WHAT...
...A BLUNDER! I...
Despair
...MAY NEVER SEE MR. TSURUGA'S BARE SKIN AGAAAAIN!

WHY DID I FORCE MYSELF TO ONLY LOOK AT HIS FACE?!
I should've looked OTHER PLACES!
Kyoko, you fool, you fool! You coward!
WHY DIDN'T YOU HAVE THE GUTS TO LOOK AT HIM ALL OVER?!
In agony
Aaa——rgh!
A traditional Japanese girl who's mad at herself for not staring at a naked man's body.
Wearing the model version of the doll mask
I'D FANTASIZED...
No...
...IMAGINED THINGS TO CREATE THE MR. TSURUGA DOLL, AND I COULD'VE MADE IT MORE REALISTIC IF I'D ACTUALLY LOOKED AT HIM!
Exactly like the real thing!
Aaaaaah!
She gets totally absorbed in projects. A typical blood type B.
ka chak

YOU'RE AL-READY DONE?
OH.
Cain.
squeak squeak
Prim
Polish-ing a ladle
...
WELL ...
I DON'T MIND...
...CUZ I WON'T HAVE TO HEAT UP THE SOUP AGAIN.
So please.
roll flop
Heeeey!
...
A late dinner
I'M NOT HUNGRY.
No!
Eat a Little, even if you're not!
NO, NOT THIS LATE.
23:45

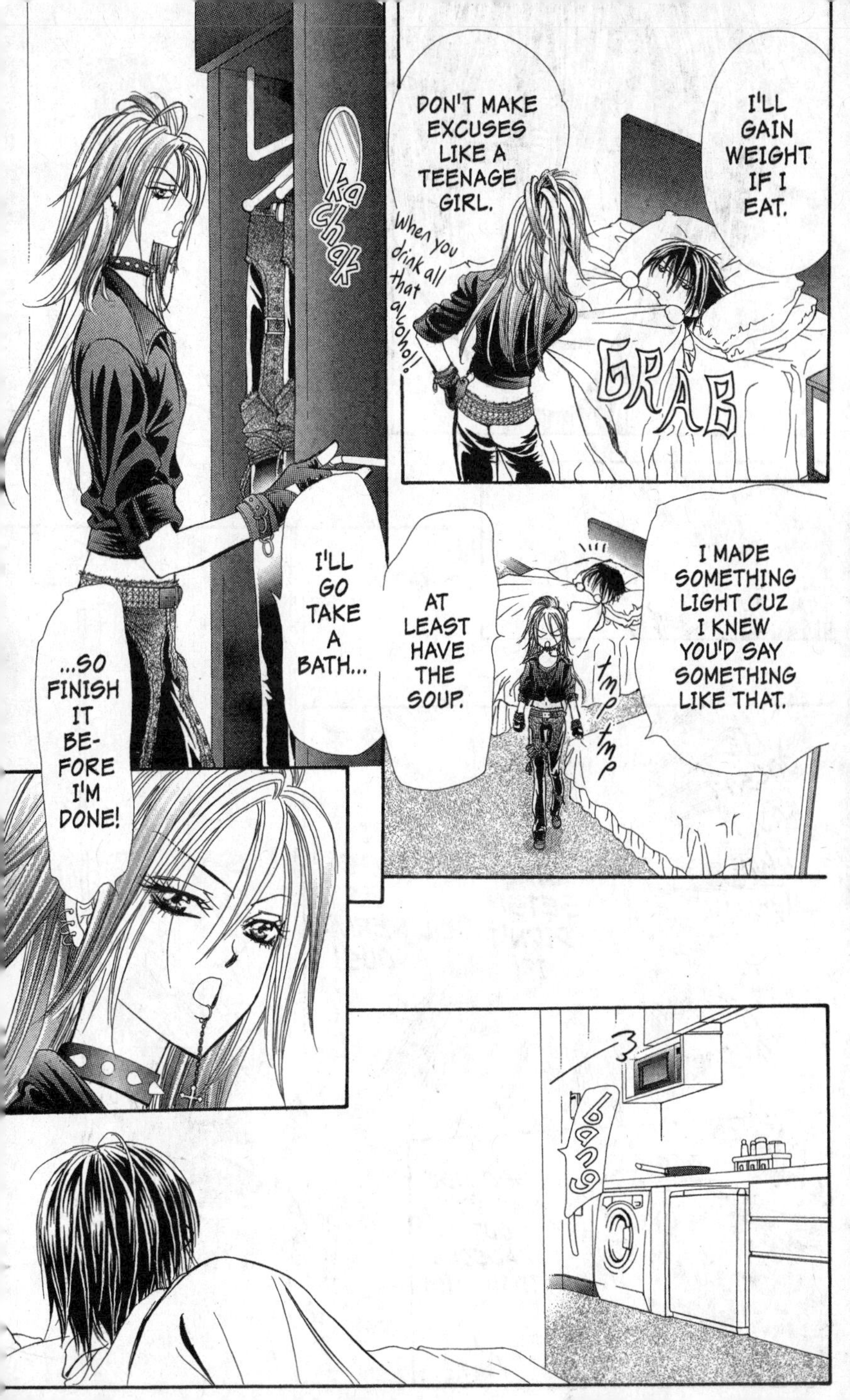
I'LL GAIN WEIGHT IF I EAT.
DON'T MAKE EXCUSES LIKE A TEENAGE GIRL.
When you drink all that alcohol!
GRAB
kachak
I MADE SOMETHING LIGHT CUZ I KNEW YOU'D SAY SOMETHING LIKE THAT.
tmp tmp
AT LEAST HAVE THE SOUP.
I'LL GO TAKE A BATH...
...SO FINISH IT BE-FORE I'M DONE!
bang

Si——gh
SKOOTCH
AAAAAAH!
Shee——sh.
I WAS SO NERVOUS!
I DID FINE! I ACTED LIKE SETSU, DIDN'T I?!
He doesn't know I was writhing in agony...
...BECAUSE OF MY OUTRAGEOUS THOUGHTS!
I-I'm so embarrassed——!
Aagh!

I'M SO EMBAR-RASSED, I CAN'T EVEN EAT TOGETHER WITH HIM!
AND I USED MY WAITRESS SOUL TO GET THROUGH IT RIGHT NOW!
It
smile
A manual for dealing with drunk customers.
Some parts have been revised for Setsu.
SURE.
IF I WASN'T COOK-ING...
...I'D LOVE TO!♡
TAKE YOUR TIME.
A per-fect wait-ress' line
SORRY, I THOUGHT YOU MIGHT'VE FALLEN ASLEEP ...
...AND GOT A LITTLE TOO WOR-RIED.
BUT NOW I FEEL SO EMBARRASSED AND ASHAMED, I'VE GOTTA COOL MY HEAD TO GET BACK IN SHAPE!
ACK ...
Oh no...
sigh...
shfff
WHEN DID I BECOME SUCH A PERVERT?
HMM ?

Cain's clothes
...
DOES THIS...
... MEAN ...
..."YOU SEND THEM OUT FOR CLEANING OR WASH THEM YOURSELF."
IS...
...THAT WHAT HE'S IMPLYING?
NO, NO.
I don't mind.
I'LL DO IT.
Of course.
THAT'S MY JOB AS YOUR SISTER.
slip...
OH...
HMM?
PLOP
MR. TSURUGA FORGOT HIS WATCH.
He shouldn't have put it in his glove...

OH?

A WATCH?

UH... THIS IS THE ONE MR. TSURUGA ALWAYS WEARS...

... RIGHT?

Probably.

OH?

WHY...

IT'S HERE BECAUSE ...

MR. TSURUGA...

...DOESN'T WEAR HIS PERSONAL STUFF WHEN HE'S WORKING.

...WAS HE WEARING IT?

IS IT BECAUSE THE FILMING HASN'T BEGUN YET?

THEN WHY?

HMM?

OH?

THIS WATCH...

2:13?

...HAS STOP-PED...

...AT...

...A STRANGE TIME...

End of Act 160

Skip·Beat!
Act 161: Violence Mission, Phase 6.5

AT LEAST HAVE THE SOUP.

I'LL GO TAKE A BATH...
...SO FINISH IT BEFORE I'M DONE!
Before I'm done!
...
...
...
roll
shuff
slow
slow
slow
clink

...

I FORGOT ...

HGRU

I...

...THE WATCH...

GLOOM
...
WAS IT...
...SUCH A BLOW?
MORE...
...THAN I'D THOUGHT...

It's here now.

THAT SHE...
...RE-SPONDED...
...SO COOLY...

EVEN IF SHE WAS ACTING...

...I THOUGHT...

...SHE'D...
...BE MORE FLUS-TERED.

...SO THE "ACCIDENTAL" CAN NEVER HAPPEN...

THIS MEANS...

...THAT SHE DOESN'T SEE ME AS A MAN AT ALL...

DEPRESSED

WELL... I SHOULD'VE KNOWN...

I KNEW IT AL-READY...

...BUT SHE COULD'VE AT LEAST BLUSHED...

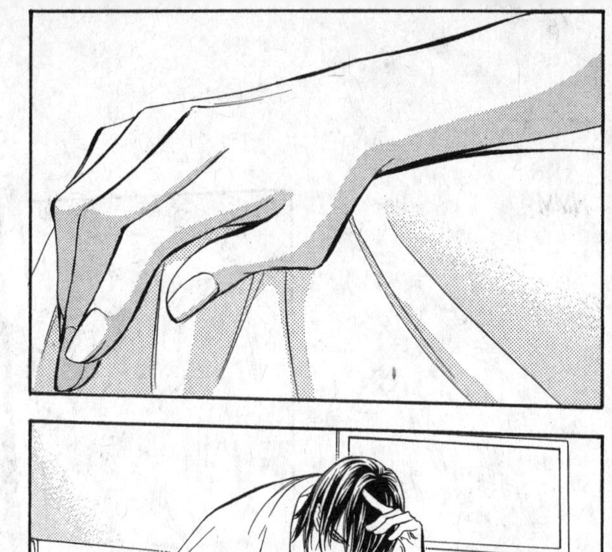

THIS...
...IS NOT GOOD ...

TO FORGET ...
...MY WATCH ...
tak
...
HMM ...

PLOP
HMM...
SOOOOOME-THING...
...IS WRONG.
With how I look.
I THOUGHT THE BATH-ROBE WOULD DO JUST FINE...
But now that I'm wearing it...
IT'S NOT LIKE SETSU.
BUT...
...WEAR-ING MY CLOTHES...
...AFTER A BATH WOULD BE WEIRD.
I mean, I wanna relax.
YET...
...WHAT I FEEL IS BEST FOR SETSU AFTER A BATH IS...

...GOING OUT LIKE THIS...
Cute But lewd cami
Cute But lewd panties
...IT'S...
...EMBARRASSIIIIIIIING!
NOOOOOOOOOOOOOOOO
YYYYYYYYY!
And, and this underwear looks so dirty
Ten got them for her.
HOW CAN I BE SO IMPROPER...
Don't look here.
Don't look here.
...IN FRONT OF A MAN...
...IN FRONT OF MR. TSURUGAAAAAA?!
I don't have the guts to do iiiiiit!

But but!
IT'S JUST LIKE SETSU TO WALK BOLDLY IN FRONT OF HER BROTHER LIKE THIS!
Cuz cuz they probably sleep in the same bed, they probably take baths together, they're that sort of creepy brother-and-sister!
Running away from reality
...SPACE ALIENS WOULD INVADE EARTH SO I DON'T HAVE TO BE SETSU ANYMOOOOOORE!
Ah, but in that case, a small country like Japan wouldn't be invaded first...
So it'd be too laaaate!
AAAAAAH, UUUUUUH, SHEEEEESH!
I WISH...

Pat
FLAP
I KNOW!
SHUP
I GOT IT!
EVEN MR. TSURUGA, WHO DOESN'T USE HIS PERSONAL ITEMS WHILE ACTING...
SHUP
...IS USING HIS OWN WATCH!
EVEN MR. TSURUGA HAS TRACES OF "MR. TSURUGA" LEFT IN HIS ACTING...
CUZ THE FILMING HASN'T BEGUN YET.
...SO I CAN LEAVE TRACES OF MYSELF TOO!
YES, AT LEAST MY PANTS, MY PANTS.
HOP
HOP
A TEENAGE GIRL MUST NOT EXPOSE THE LOWER HALF OF HER BODY!
I'LL BE FINE! HE WON'T GET ANGRY OR SIGH THAT MY ACTING IS NO GOOD!

huddled
EVEN IF IT'S NOT LIKE SETSU, WHO LOVES TO DRESS UP!
Wearing clothes she's already worn (should go straight to the wash pile)
IS IT A CO-COON?
Cain
I SEE...
SO, CAIN SLEEPS LIKE THIS.
Phew
OH...
IF HE'S ASLEEP...
...I DIDN'T HAVE TO WORRY SO MUCH ABOUT WHAT I WORE AFTER MY BATH...
Oh!
I KNOW.
A HOTEL USUALLY HAS YUKATA!
I was so flustered, I'd completely forgotten!
YES! HOW ABOUT SETSU IN A YUKATA?
And I'M used to that too!
She wore them instead of pajamas when she was in Kyoto

SETSU MIGHT LOOK BETTER IN THAT THAN IN A BATH-ROBE!
They didn't have a yukata...
...
The hotel logo
mumble mumble
A stylish outlaw Girl would NOT wear this!
And my brother wouldn't either!
I'LL GET SOMETHING ON MY WAY TO WORK TOMORROW FOR SETSU'S NIGHTWEAR.
TOMOR-ROW?
Hmm?
...BUT WHAT ABOUT MR. TSURU-GA?
HAS HE FINISHED FILMING THE LAST EPISODE OF DARK MOON?
Mio finished around Valen-tine's
OH?
WORK?
I HAVE BOX R AT 10 TOMORROW ...
CUZ MIO WILL ALSO BE ON SET ON THE LAST DAY.
They were going to tell me when the date is set...
NO... PROB-ABLY NOT...

tick
click click
click click
YES.
HELLO?
flip
Ah.

Excuse me for calling you so late. It's Mogami.

HI.

WHY'RE YOU CALLING ME SO LATE?

Uh

E-Excuse me...

You must've been asleep...

Huh?

NO.

I'M STILL AWAKE.

SO WHAT'S UP? SOMETHING WRONG?

Um... I'm calling...

...about Mr. Tsuruga's work schedule.

Will you tell me his schedule for tomorrow on?

UH.

I'D GLADLY TELL HER...

Since it's Kyoko asking.

?

Um... Mr. Yashiro?

But...

HE'S STARTING THE MOVIE SHOOT IN A WEEK...

...AND STARTS HIS DOUBLE LIFE AS ACTOR X... CAIN HEEL.

THE IDENTITY OF CAIN HEEL IS A SECRET...
...SO I CAN'T RISK HAVING SOMEONE FIND OUT ABOUT IT...
Uh...
SORRY, SORRY.
EVEN IF IT IS KYOKO...
Uh...
WHY?
Wha?
SILENCE
HMM?
Oh?
I'm sorry. I'm out of line. Goodbye.
THAT'S HOW SHE REACTED BEFORE...
HELLO?
UUUM.
YOU WANT TO KNOW REN'S SCHEDULE?
Yes.
SORRY, KYOKO.
KYOKO?
Y-You all right? You there?
...
...
Mr. Yashiro ...
Ah
SHE'S THERE.

Maybe... you...
...don't know?
HUH?
ABOUT WHAT?
That I'm...
...acting as...
...Mr. Tsuruga's... Cain Heel's younger sister...
bip
...
...MR. YASHIRO WAS AWFULLY EXCITED...
FOR SOME REASON...
I WONDER WHY...?
WHEN HE'S MR. TSURUGA'S MANAGER...
BUT HE DIDN'T SEEM TO KNOW.
...
MAYBE...
...ME BEING MR. TSURUGA'S "GOOD-LUCK CHARM"...
...TODAY...
...IT'S ALREADY YESTERDAY...
...WAS JUST A WHIM OF THE PRESIDENT'S?

Yes.
NOW THAT I THINK ABOUT IT...
...HE DID SAY SOMETHING LIKE "THEN I'D LIKE TO TAKE THIS OPPOR-TUNITY."
THE MUSE FIRST TOLD ME WHAT SETSU IS LIKE.
The muse of magic, Magical Ten
Her magic items
IF THE PRESIDENT THOUGHT OF IT OUT OF THE BLUE, THE MUSE WOULDN'T HAVE KNOWN EITHER.
Oh?
BUT THEN, THE PRE-PARATIONS FOR SETSU WERE PRETTY THOROUGH.
tmp tmp
Hmm...
...THIS WAS PLANNED?
MAY-BE...
HMM?
...
WELL...
rustle
AT LEAST HE ATE SOMETHING. THAT'S GOOD.
I'LL HAVE SOME SALAD AND GET SOME SLEEP.
clink clank
TOMORROW I'LL WAKE MR. TSURUGA AT 7:30, MAKE HIM EAT BREAK-FAST...
...AND TAKE HIM TO THE MUSE.
Miss Woods will have a temporary beauty salon ready in the underground parking garage of the hotel at 8AM.

SO TOMORROW MR. TSURUGA MUST BE ON THE DARK MOON SET AT 10AM.

Sheesh

HE DOESN'T TELL ME ANYTHING.

OF COURSE, IT'D BE WEIRD TALKING ABOUT REN TSURUGA'S SCHEDULE WHILE WE'RE ACTING LIKE THE HEEL BROTHER AND SISTER.

squeak squeak

I WAS COMMANDED TO TAKE THIS ROLE FOR GREATER SAFETY, AS SOMEONE WHO KNOWS WHAT'S GOING ON.

IF I DON'T KNOW ANYTHING, I CAN'T PROTECT CAIN HEEL'S SECRETS!

Pout

wsh wsh wsh

I KNOW MR. TSURUGA CAN GET TO WORK EVEN IF I DON'T WAKE HIM UP.

I'm just here to feed him.

BUT I HAVE MY DUTIES.

wsh wsh

She's only washing the light clothes

wsh wsh

bounce

bounce
bounce

bounce
bounce

...

bounce
bounce
bounce
bounce

amble
amble

tmp
tmp

IT'S BECAUSE YOU DIDN'T DRY YOUR HAIR, AND FELL ASLEEP BURIED IN THE COMFORTER!

MY HAIR ALWAYS BOUNCES.

Bouncing for style
Bedhead
Bouncing for style
Bouncing for style
Bedhead
Bedhead

IT'S BOUNCING FOR A REASON.

IT'S BEDHEAD.

N-o.

ka chak
WELL, I THINK THE MUSE WILL FIX IT TODAY...
AH.
Hiiiiiii!♡
Morn-ing, you two.
?!
TH-THE MUSE?!
It's her pretty voice!
thu-thump
Heh heh
I DRESSED UP SO I'D BLEND IN WITH YOU TWO.
B2
This way.
DON'T I LOOK GOOD?
Y...
Yes, you do!

YOU LOOK DIFFER-ENT, BUT YOU LOOK GREAT!
You ARE a muse of magic.
Ooh!
Thanks! ♡
Ah.
IT'S OVER THERE.
IT LOOKS LIKE A TRAILER.
My temporary Beauty salon.
!
Oh!
Well...
IT'S NOT THAT BIG...
...BUT IT'S BIG ENOUGH FOR FOUR OF US.
FOUR?
Hmm?
WELL...
...COME IN.
kachak

YO, THE HEEL SIBLINGS.
We just met yesterday.

HAVE YOU GOTTEN COZY WITH EACH OTHER?
grin
Lory Takarada
Today's costume:
A villainous underground broker
He's my guy!

Ooh... my darling looks great in anything! ♡
The president looks plain...

KYOOOKOOO.

HERE.

THIS...
Is your work uniform.

Ah.

THANK YOU.

ARE YOU REALLY WEAR-ING THIS TO WORK?

I DON'T HAVE ANYTHING ELSE THAT I CAN WEAR TODAY...

...AND I'M SCARED I MIGHT BE LATE IF I GO HOME FIRST...

SOME-THING WRONG?

NO...
...VOWED TO GOD THAT I'D...
...NEVER HURT SOMEONE AGAIN.
I...
SO...

...IT WAS...

...SUP-POSED TO BE...

...A HEAVY, HEAVY SHACKLE...

...THE WATCH EXISTED...

I...

...DON'T NEED...

End of Act 161

tmp

tmp

tmp

tmp

AH...

tmp

tmp

pmph

MORN-
ING...

Skip·Beat!

Act 162: Violence Mission, Phase 7

I heeeaaard abooooUT iiiiiiT.
Now let's play with Ren!
... LIVING WITH KYOOOKOOOOOOOO?
Pffft
YOU'RE ...
I CAN'T HELP BUT CRY WITH PITY AS A FELLOW MAN.
chuckle
LIVING UNDER THE SAME ROOF WITH THE GIRL YOU'RE IN LOVE WITH!
Sweet traps rolling all over! There's no way the fake brother and sister setup can hold you back!
IT'S ...
...THE ULTIMATE TOOORTUUURE!
Ah sheesh. Poor Re~~~n!
Kyah
Kyah
fwip fwip
...

HMM.
FROM WHAT I HEARD FROM MS. MOGAMI THIS MORNING, HE DOES KNOW ABOUT IT...
LAST NIGHT I CALLED MR. YASHIRO AND ASKED ABOUT YOUR SCHEDULE.
HE'S NOT TEASING ME ABOUT CAIN AND SETSU AT ALL.
THEN ...
...HE ASKED ME WHAT WAS GOING ON, AND HE SEEMED VERY EXCITED.
Why?
He's your manager...
DIDN'T MR. YASHIRO KNOW ABOUT THE HEELS?
I DIDN'T TELL YASHIRO ABOUT SETSU.
AH YES.

YOU KNOW, TO REALLY KEEP A SECRET ...
... PEOPLE SAY...
Yet...
...YOU MUST FIRST DUPE YOUR ALLIES.
Oh no
I-I'M SORRY. WHAT... HAVE I DONE?!
AH, SO WHAT. YOU TOLD HIM ABOUT IT.
I wonder if things will be okay...
Hmm...
THINGS WILL BE FINE. HE'S JUST LYING.
He's so sure
SHEESH... MS. MOGAMI IS GETTING DUPED AGAIN...
YOU GOTTA BE MORE SUS-PICIOUS OF THE PRESI-DENT.
Like...
HE JUST THOUGHT OF IT CUZ IT SOUNDED FUN.
OR...
MEN'S
...THERE'S A SERIOUS REASON BEHIND IT...
SO YOU DON'T NEED A GOOD-LUCK CHARM?
... SCARED ?
HMM?
WHAT IS IT...?
ARE YOU...

THAT YOU WON'T BE ABLE TO KEEP ACTING AS HER BROTHER?

Hey, hey what's going on. You've only spent one night with her.

IS YOUR WILL-POWER WORN-OUT LIKE A RUBBER BAND?

It breaks as soon as you pull on it.

NO.

Then...

IS IT A PIECE OF TWISTED PAPER?

Twisted piece of paper

I AM NOT TALKING ABOUT MY WILLPOWER.

...

ALTHOUGH ...

...THAT MAY HAVE SOMETHING TO DO WITH IT...

WHICH IS IT?

WHEN SHE'S WITH ME...
...I NEARLY FORGET...
... WHAT I...

...MUST REMEMBER IN ORDER TO LIVE...

REEEEEN?
He~y, I'm here. Snap out of it.
Oh!
wave wave

WHA ?
Oh.
YOU'RE BACK.
THEY'RE READY, SO YOU CAN GO NOW.
AH ...
bow

YES.
I'M COMING.
chak
MEN'S
PRESS
shp
YOU ALL RIGHT?
WHA?
WHAT DO YOU MEAN?
WELL...
I THOUGHT MAYBE YOU WEREN'T ABLE TO SLEEP... LAST NIGHT.

I WOULDN'T BE SUR-PRISED.
He's whisper-ing.
BEING ALONE IN A SMALL HOTEL ROOM WITH THE GIRL YOU LOVE.
SHE'S SO CLOSE, YOU COULD TOUCH HER IF YOU HAPPEN TO EXTEND YOUR HAND.
YOU'D NEED TO MUSTER ALL YOUR WILLPOWER TO CONTROL YOURSELF IF SHE FELL ASLEEP, COMPLETELY DEFENSELESS.

JUST IMAGINING IT...
...MAKES ME CRY WITH PITY AS A FELLOW MAN.
What a cruel torture this is...
HE'S SERI-OUSLY PITYING ME!
This is depressing.
I'M SORRY... I GOT CARRIED AWAY LAST NIGHT CUZ THIS WAS SOMEBODY ELSE'S PROBLEM...
I WISH HE'D SMILE LIKE ALWAYS AND TEASE ME ABOUT IT.

I'M DOING MY BEST NOT TO THINK ABOUT THAT SORT OF THING BY CONCENTRATING ON MY ROLE...
But you're forcing me to remember!
WELL, I CAN UNDERSTAND WHY THE PRESIDENT WOULD BE SO WORRIED ABOUT LEAVING YOU ALONE.
SINCE CAIN HEEL WOULD CARE FOR HIMSELF EVEN LESS THAN REN.
clip
clop
clip

BUT IF YOU KEEP NOT BEING ABLE TO SLEEP, I'M AFRAID YOU MIGHT END UP COLLAPSING.
Even if you're tough.
PEOPLE CAN SURVIVE A FEW DAYS WITHOUT EATING, BUT THEY DIE FROM LACK OF SLEEP.
tmp
REN...
whisper
YOU'RE NOT APPEARING IN THE MOVIE AS A BROTHER AND SISTER.
KYOKO ACCEPTED THIS AS A LOVE ME ASSIGN-MENT...
...SO SHE'S NOT GETTING PAID TO ACT AS YOUR SISTER.

EVEN IF YOUR "SISTER" DISAPPEARS RIGHT NOW...
...IT WON'T CAUSE ANY PROB-LEMS.
TO BE HON-EST...
...YOUR FEELINGS FOR KYOKO ASIDE...
...IF YOU FIND YOUR CURRENT SITUATION DIFFICULT TO DEAL WITH...
YOU...
...SHOULD CONSIDER IT AS AN OPTION.
I DON'T MIND.
IF YOU'RE FINDING THINGS DIFFICULT...
...WE CAN PRETEND YOUR "SISTER" NEVER EXISTED.
CRUSH

BUT YOU'RE ...

... GONNA HAVE TO FIRE MS. MOGAMI YOURSELF.
WHAAAT?!
WH...

WHY DO I...

CUZ YOU SAID YOU DON'T NEED HER.

I REFUSE TO GO ALONG WITH IT.

I THINK YOU NEED THAT GIRL...

... BUT ...

...YOU DO HAVE THE FINAL SAY.

SHE WON'T BE CONVINCED IF YOU'RE CONSIDERATE AND SAY THINGS YOU DON'T MEAN...

...SO ELL HER XACTLY WHAT OU'RE HINKING.

grin
"I...
...SIMPLY DON'T NEED YOU."
"SO YOU DON'T NEED TO SHOW UP ANYMORE."
JUST LIKE THAT.
WHAT...

...SORT OF SHADY ORGANI-ZATION DOES THAT MAN BELONG TO?
Seriously...
THIS ISN'T FAIR.

HE SAID THAT, KNOWING I CAN NEVER SAY SOMETHING LIKE THAT TO HER.
SINCE I NEED HER...

BESIDES, I DON'T HATE THE SITUATION I'M IN.

IT'S JUST IT CAN BE INCONVENIENT SOMETIMES.
Yes, in many ways...

...NOT CON-FIDENT.

WILL I BE ABLE TO STOP MYSELF NEXT TIME...

...BEFORE I GO BERSERK?

WILL I BE ABLE TO STOP MYSELF...

THE SCHEDULE HAS CHANGED...
...SO PLEASE ADJUST ACCORD-INGLY.
Ye——s!
Oh!
!
THEN TSURUGA, MS. MOMOSE, KIJIMA. PLEASE.
Yes.
disperse
disperse
...
Yeeees.
...
DARN...

...NOW THAT THE SHACKLES ARE GONE?

I...

...WASN'T LISTENING AGAIN...

AND SO...

Blah
Blah
Blah
Blah
Blah Blah
whisper whisper
HEY.
WHY WON'T YOU SAY ANY-THING?!
I KNOW YOU GUYS WERE BULLYING KUMIKO!
San!
IF YOU DON'T WANT ME GOING TO THE POLICE, YOU COME TO THE HOSPITAL RIGHT NOW...
...AND APOLOGIZE TO MY YOUNGER SISTER!
SHE SAID.
Peek
I...
... DON'T MIND.

blink
CUZ...
Arte
shuul
...I'VE GOT TIME...
shff
shff

HMM?
Cut.

Blah
Blah
Blah
Blah
WEEELL.
IT WASN'T BAD...

WELL IF YOU UNDER-STAND, YOU'LL BE ABLE TO DO FINE NEXT TIME.
YES, OF COURSE!
I WILL!

...BUT... IT DIDN'T REALLY FEEL LIKE NATSU.
You had this blank look on your face, and were too low-key.
YOU'RE RIGHT... I'M SORRY.
NATSU WOULD SMILE HAPPILY WHILE SAYING HER LINES...
YUP.

ALL RIGHT, THEN WE'LL DO IT ONE MORE TIIIIME.
Ye~~~s
DARN ...
...I WAS SETSU...
THE MOMENT I THOUGHT THAT...
No, no. Do your best, Natsu. Don't have your body taken over so easily!
Phew
THAT WASN'T GOOD...
FOR A MOMENT ...
"SETSU...
...WOULD LOVE THIS LIP GLOSS."
tap tap
clink
UM, NATSU WOULD PREFER THIS SORT OF COLOR.
...
TO BE TAKEN OVER BY ANOTHER ROLE WHILE ACTING...
Scene 17, once more.
THAT WAS A SURPRISE...
Ready...
shf
I GUESS...
...I WASN'T ABLE TO COMPLETELY SWITCH INTO NATSU...

...action!

I'M...

...a little...

...DISAP-POINTED IN MYSELF ...

I'M REALLY ...

...DISAP-POINTED ...

...THAT YOU LOVE TO WEAR GAUDY UNDERWEAR LIKE A CARNIVOROUS FEMALE...

I was sure you were more modest...

I feel betrayed...

Wah

Cute but lewd panties

Cute but lewd lingerie

What am I doing ?!

OH.
SO THEY'RE GIFTS FOR SOMEONE.
WELL ... YES... W...
Heh heh
I BOUGHT ALL OF THEM FOR SETSU.
They're gifts, gifts.
THOUGH I'LL BE WEARING THEM.
But that me isn't me...
She ended up buying them.
ARE YOU GIVING THAT GIFT...
...TO THE OTHER LOVE ME MEMBER?
Wha?
Moko won't wear such dirty and lewd underwear!
She's got fashion sense and is elegant!
She saw Moko's underwear at the training school.
THEY ARE DIRTY AND LEWD.
WHAT SORT OF PERSON WEARS THAT SORT OF UNDERWEAR?
She's so curious
Uh...
U... um...
A HARD-ROCK GIRL WITH A SOUL OF FIRE WHO LOVES TO DRESS UP...
...
Argh
...
stare
DID IT SOUND UNNATURAL?
B...
BUT BUT, I CAN'T TELL HER THE TRUTH!
And I've already accidentally let Mr. Yashiro in on the secret...
KYOKO ...

YOU'RE A STRANGE ONE.
chuckle
YOU'RE FRIENDS WITH THAT SORT OF PEOPLE TOO?
DID YOU GET TO KNOW HER THROUGH A LOVE ME ASSIGNMENT?
...
U...
UH... YES.
S... Sort... of...
Oh.
MY SENIOR IS WALKING THERE ON FOOT...
...SO I CAN'T JUST HOP INTO A CAR AND LEAVE.
Hmm...
...
I... SEE...
HMM...
Um
MS. AMA-MIYA.
By the way...
WHY'RE YOU WALKING TO OUR NEXT LOCATION?
WHA?
HUH?
Your senior?

YOU'RE MY SENIOR...
...IN THE LOVE ME SEC-TION.
WHAAAA?!
N-NO, JUST BECAUSE I JOINED A YEAR AND FEW DAYS BEFORE YOU?!

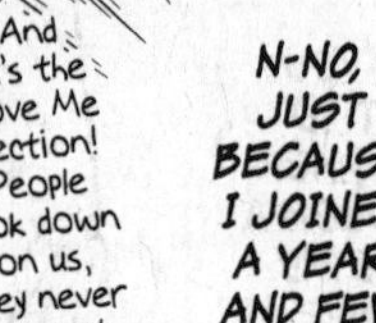
And it's the Love Me section! People look down on us, they never respect us!
How can this be pos-sible?!

MS. AMAMIYA, YOU'RE MY SENIOR IN SHOWBIZ, A REAL PRO!
BESIDES, WE'RE GOING TO THE PARK RIGHT OVER THERE.
Look, we can see it now.

I'LL BE THERE WHILE I'M WAITING FOR THE CAR TO PICK ME UP.
AND...
...I'M TAKING A BREAK ANYWAY...

...SO I FIGURED I'D WALK TO CLEAR MY MIND.
WHA?

I...
...USED TO BE IN TURMOIL NO MATTER WHAT I DID...

BUT...

..."CHIORI AMAMIYA" WAS A STAGE ACTRESS UNTIL JUST RECENTLY...

...AND IT'S ONLY BEEN FOUR YEARS SINCE SHE'S MADE HER DEBUT.

EVEN IF I AM AN ACTRESS...

Why won't anybody notice me?! An ACTRESS is walking! I'm not an actress who just made her debut! Sheesh, everyone, everyone is stupid! Your memories are worse than a monkey's cuz you don't use your brains! But if a human-like being had some old memories left and realized I used to be Akari Tendo, I'll push them off the station platform twice!

LIKE THIS...

It's my bitter female feelings that I want to be noticed, but don't really want to be noticed...

How could she say this on New Year's Day?!

WHAT A TERROR-IST DICTATOR SHE IS! SHE'S DROWNING IN RAGE!

NOOOOOOOO

Chiori's rage diary. The date is New Year's Day last year, when she visited a shrine.

Sigh

AND THAT'S ...

...OF COURSE THE PUBLIC WOULDN'T NOTICE ME.
ding dong
Blah
Blah
Blah Blah
SHE'S A NEW-COMER...
...OF SORTS.

click
... HOW ...
...I DECIDED I'D LOOK AT THINGS.

YES.
NOT HAVING PEOPLE RECOGNIZE ME MEANS I CAN BE FREE.
For instance...
EVEN IF I BOUGHT EMBAR-RASSING UNDERWEAR LIKE YOU...
...
...NO ONE WOULD NOTICE AND MAKE WEIRD RUMORS ABOUT IT!
Yes, now I can do all sorts of things I couldn't do in the past!
I...
...
... DON'T QUITE UNDER-STAND ...
Ugh...
NOW I REAL-IZE WHAT I DIDN'T WANT TO...
People should know your face and name thanks to DARK MOON...
WHY DOESN'T ANYBODY NOTICE YOU?
Now that I think about it...
UH.
Oh?

...BUT WHEN I'M NOT ACTING ...
Not acting
...MOST PEOPLE DON'T REALIZE I'M THE ONE WHO PLAYS MIO.
THE ONLY TIME I APPEARED ON TELEVISION DRESSED LIKE THIS WAS THAT QUIZ SHOW.
...
EVEN MORE WHEN I LOOK LIKE THIS.
I THINK ...
...RIGHT NOW I DON'T LOOK LIKE "KYOKO" OR "MIO." I'M SOMEONE ELSE ENTIRELY ...
...SO I'M LIKE A NAMELESS NEWCOMER TOO.
Actually, people might not think I'm an actress at all.
FAIRY...
What?!
Where?!
Where ...
... where ?!
Where is it?!
So excited

KYA—H!!
Hmm?
REALLY?!
REALLY?!
SQUEE
SQUEE
YOU'RE SERIOUS, YOU'RE SERIOUS?!
SQUEE SQUEE
YEAH! YEAH!
I SAW HIM COME OUT OF THAT CAR!
Pop
Pop
ZOOM
Must be that way!
A Ferrari
Wha?
UH HEY, KYOKO–
HE'S HIDING BEHIND THE CAR, BUT I'M 100% TOTALLY SURE!
Totally and 100%?!
SQUEEEEEE!
SQUEEEEEEE! I can't believe it!
TH...
TH-THUMP TH-THUMP
...THAT ALL THESE PEOPLE ARE WITNESSING IT!
What sort of klutzy fairy are you?!
I can't believe it!
Ah!
He's there!
SHOOM
...THAT LIVES IN THE CITY!
I WANNA SEE IT! THE FAIRY...
I don't care if it's a low-level, klutzy, no-good fairy!
Just joking!
NO, NO NO, JUST JOKING!

SEE? IT'S...
...REN TSURUGA AAAA!
...THE REAL ...
End of Act 162

Skip·Beat!
Act 163: Violence Mission, Phase 7.5

I'M LOOKING FOR AN IMMORTAL BUTTERFLY.

AS THE NAME IMPLIES, IT'S A BUTTERFLY THAT LIVES FOREVER.

IT HAS TRANSPARENT, COLORLESS WINGS.
IT DOESN'T GLOW. IT'S NOT FLASHY AT ALL.
IT SITS STILL...
...AND LIVES BY TRICKING OUR HUMAN EYES.

THE BUTTERFLY DANCES WITH DIFFERENT COLORS DEPENDING ON THE TIME AND PLACE...
A PASSION-ATE CRIMSON.
A CLEAR BLUE.
A DULL EARTH TONE THAT CAN'T BE CALLED BEAUTIFUL.
...AND HUMANS FORTUNATE ENOUGH TO SEE IT...
...NEVER...
...REALIZE IT'S THE SAME BUTTERFLY EACH TIME.
IT HIDES ITS REAL SELF.
IT HIDES ITS EXIS-TENCE.
WHEN YOU'RE ABLE TO RECOGNIZE THE "ESSENCE" OF THAT BUTTERFLY WITHOUT BEING FOOLED BY ITS EVER-CHANGING WINGS...
...THE "IMMORTAL BUTTERFLY" AS I NAMED IT, MIGHT THEN BE CALLED...
...A "FAIRY"...
...AS PEOPLE KNOW IT.

I AM STILL LOOKING FOR IT...

...IN THIS WORLD OF SHOWBIZ, A FAIRYTALE REALM THAT ACTUALLY EXISTS.
SOMEONE WHO CAN KEEP TRANSFORMING WHEN GIVEN AN EXISTENCE CALLED A ROLE.

A HUMAN BEING WITH TRANS-PARENT...

AN IMMORTAL BUTTER-FLY...

...COLOR-
LESS
WINGS....

GET THE
VICTORY MARK

...MIGHT HAVE FOUND ONE.

MY DEAR MASTER.

THE FATHER OF VICTORY, MR. D.

Squeee~ Squeee~

THE "IMMORTAL BUTTER-FLY" YOU'VE BEEN LOOK-ING FOR...

Squeee~ Squeee~

Squeee squeee~

...

HMM?

POP

IS THAT...

...THE DARK MOON SHOOT?

THAT'S REN TSURUGA OVER THERE.

That's why all the girls and women are making such a fuss.

Squeee~ Squeee~ Squeee~

UH...

LOOKS LIKE IT.
THERE'RE CAR CHASES IN THE FINAL EPISODE, SO I THINK THIS MUST BE IT.
HMM.
UH... WHAT?
DID THE LAST EPISODE OF TSUKIGOMORI HAVE A CHASE SCENE?
I don't remember, though I've watched it many times cuz I liked it as a child.

NO, THIS HAPPENS ONLY IN DARK MOON.
THEY CHANGED THE STORY A LITTLE STARTING IN THE MIDDLE.
Ah.
I SEE.
She hasn't been watching recent dramas, cuz they piss her off.
Ah.
Oh nooooooo.
IS MR. TSURUGA DOING THE STUNTS HIMSELF?
I THINK SO...
...SINCE MR. TSURUGA WANTS TO DO EVERYTHING HIMSELF...
I can't see him anymore!
Too bad.
HE MUST'VE GOTTEN IN HIS CAR AGAIN.
...
...

LET US GO.
WE'RE DIFFERENT FROM THE ORDINARY GIRLS WHO'RE LOITERING HERE.
fwip
UH ...
I DON'T WANT PEOPLE TO THINK WE'RE THE SAME AS THEM.
Why do I need to go "squee" over a fellow actor?! No way!
TROMP TROMP
...
What?!
M-MS. AMAMIYA! MAYBE ...!
SHOCK
...
TROMP TROMP
SHE HOLDS POISONOUS THOUGHTS TOWARDS SOMEONE LIKE MR. TSURUGA TOO?!

They're filming a drama!
It's Ren Tsuruga!
Woo~
dash dash
peek

U...
UM, MISS AMAMIYA...
SO WHEN CAN YOU START GETTING READY?
WHAT DID DIRECTOR OGATA SAY?
...AND SO THE DIRECTOR SAID ABOUT HALF AN HOUR AT MOST.
HALF AN HOUR... HMM...
THEY'RE GONNA NEED SOME MORE TIME FOR TRAFFIC CONTROL...
YES ...
WE ONLY HAVE PERMISSION TO SHOOT HERE FOR TWO HOURS.

WITH REHEARSAL TIME AND SETTING UP THE STREET, YOU MIGHT...

...ONLY GET ONE CHANCE TO SHOOT IT FOR REAL...

YEAH.

Well...

I'LL DO MY BEST.

...

SO YOU HAVE NO INTENTION OF USING A STUNT—

NO.

YOU MIGHT NOT EVEN BE ABLE TO REHEARSE PROPERLY.

YOU HAVE BJ AFTER THIS, SO IF YOU GET HURT...

I'LL BE FINE.

YOU WORRY TOO MUCH, MR. YASHIRO.

I'M ONLY DRIVING THE WRONG WAY AT ABOUT 60 MILES AN HOUR.
THEN I SKID MY CAR AND CRASH IT A LITTLE AGAINST NAOYUKI'S CAR TO STOP IT, CUZ MIZUKI IS IN IT.
The role Kijima's playing
chuckle
Skid and crash a little at about 60 miles an hour.

DIE FAST LIVE HARD
Did he used to be a member of the Hell's Angels?
THIS GUY...
BESIDES, ONCE I GOT THE SCRIPT FOR THIS EPISODE...
...I STARTED SECRETLY PRAC-TICING FOR THIS SCENE.
Huh?!
Practicing?!
WHEN AND WHERE WERE YOU DOING THAT?!
You gotta drive the wrong way, then skid and crash!
I MEAN, THE SCRIPT WAS ONLY READY A FEW DAYS AGO!
How much practice did did you do to make you so confident?

WELL.
JUST IMAGING.
Another name for it...
...IS FANTA-SIZING.
Are you Kyoko?!
No, no, what sort of confidence is that?!
This is even more dangerous!
shhk
UH.
TSURUGA.
ARE YOU FREE NOW?
YES? HAS SOMETHING CHANGED?
Uh...
...no.
THIS HAS NOTHING TO DO WITH WORK.
Um
SOME-ONE'S HERE TO SEE YOU.
?

Wha?

Wha~~~t?!
Kyoko? Are you really Kyoko?!
Wah~~~!
I wouldn't have recognized you!
WHY'RE YOU DRESSED LIKE THAT?!
UH...
I'M APPEARING IN ANOTHER DRAMA...

...AND THIS IS THE UNIFORM I WEAR IN IT.
I'm a high school student with charisma!
NO, NO... I WASN'T TALKING ABOUT YOUR COSTUME...
KYOKO, YOU CAN REALLY CHANGE WHEN YOU'RE IN A DIFFERENT ROLE.

YOU LOOK TWICE AS GROWN-UP AS USUAL.
And you look beautiful.
Huh?!
Really?! I'm so happy!
...
CAN YOU IMAGINE KYOKO LOOKING GROWN-UP?
And twice as much.
WHA?
HMM...
I wonder...

KNOWING HOW KYOKO USUALLY IS, I JUST CAN'T IMAGINE IT...

RIGHT?

AND "BEAUTIFUL"?
She?
An ordinary girl with no distinguishing features
fidget
ENVIOUS
fidget

HOW MUCH HAS SHE CHANGED?

Chak

Twitch

IS BOX R SHOOTING NEAR HERE?

YES.

Actually...

AT THE PARK RIGHT OVER THERE—

RIGHT.

...LET'S GO THERE.

THEN...

Wha?

ZOOM

Huh?!

3 seconds

Wha?!

D-Did he teleport?!

But he zoomed so elegantly.

WH-WHAT'S GOING ON? WHY DID REN SUDDENLY ...?
He took off like he was spiriting her away.
WAS SOMETHING WR—
AH SHEESH, I COULDN'T CATCH HER.
TSURUGA'S AWFULLY QUICK!
A big animal moves more slowly.
?!
KIJIMA?! WHEN DID HE GET HERE?!
Ha!
UH, MAYBE...
...REN ZOOMED AWAY BECAUSE OF HIM?!
SO KIJIMA WOULDN'T BE ABLE TO LOOK AT KYOKO?!
TWICE AS GROWN-UP, AND A BEAUTY.
WHAT SORT OF TRANSFORMATION HAS SHE GONE THROUGH?
HOW AM I GONNA QUIET DOWN THIS CURIOUS HEART OF MINE?
I wanted to see her...
I really wanted to...
curious
fidget
BINGO!
KIJIMA DIDN'T CARE ABOUT KYOKO AT ALL!
Yet he stood up! (From his seat!) This is a problem!
WHAT IF HE SAW HER AND GOT EVEN MORE INTERESTED IN HER!

REN...
I REALLY AM STUPEFIED.
WHEN...
...DID YOU REALIZE KIJIMA STOOD UP?!
Eye-Balls?! He's Got eyeBalls all over his Body like a Barnacle ?!
Horrified
U... U...
MR. TSURUGA.
I'M AMAZED AT YOUR ABILITY TO MANAGE DANGEROUS SITUATIONS.
SHOULD YOU HAVE LEFT JUST NOW?
DON'T WORRY. I STILL HAVE TIME.
tmp tmp
tmp tmp
OH, I SEE...

HUH
?

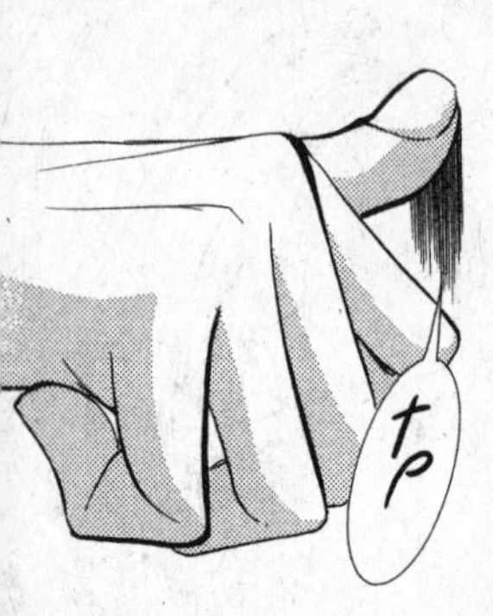
tp

THE PRINCESS ROSA...

LOOKS GOOD ON YOU.

...LOOKS GOOD ON NATSU.

!

I THINK SO TOO!

I shouldn't be saying it when I made it, but...!

UNTIL I ACTUALLY WORE IT, I WAS WORRIED THAT NATSU WOULDN'T BE GOOD ENOUGH FOR MISS PRINCESS ROSA, WHO'S SO SO BEAUTIFUL...

...BUT IT ACTUALLY LOOKS GOOD ON NATSU.

And many people tell me she's beautiful.

The Princess Rosa

Her excitement meter
100
90
80
ZOOM
AND SO...
YES?
...THAT WHEN PEOPLE CALL NATSU "GROWN-UP" AND "BEAUTIFUL"...
...I ALWAYS THINK...
...80 percent of it is due to the magic of Miss Princess Rosa!
The rest is due to the magical items Moko gave me! ※
AH HA HA.
THAT'S NOT IT.
BLUNT
※ It breaks her heart to re-buy the items she's used up, but she does.
ZOOOOM
...THAT YOU LOOK COMPLETELY DIFFERENT FROM THE USUAL YOU OR MIO.
Well...
So...
IT'S THANKS TO PRINCESS ROSA AND MOKO'S—
mumble mumble
...I WAS A LITTLE SUR-PRISED TOO...
TO BE HONEST ...
YOU CAN TRANSFORM YOURSELF TO SUIT YOUR ROLE, AND I FEEL 80 PERCENT OF THAT IS THANKS TO THE TALENTS YOU WERE BORN WITH.

YOU'RE
...

...REALLY—
BY THE WAY, MR. TSURUGA.

...
Ren's tossed-aside word.
REALLY
WHA?
YOU'RE ...
...DOING THE CAR STUNTS YOURSELF.

UH... YES.

I PLAN TO DO THEM MYSELF ...

I KNEW YOU...
...WOULDN'T USE A STUNTMAN, BUT...

OF COURSE ... YOU WOULD ...

ARE YOU WORRIED ABOUT ME?

CUZ... JUST DRIVING FAST ISN'T ENOUGH.

WHEN I RECEIVED THE SCRIPT FOR THE LAST EPISODE...
...I THOUGHT ABOUT GETTING A GOOD-LUCK CHARM FOR YOU...
Hand-made of course
...BUT I DE-CIDED NOT TO.
WHAT?
Really?
THAT'S TOO BAD.
I WOULD'VE WANTED ONE.
No way!
YELL
No way?
HOW COULD YOU SO MERCI-LESSLY...
I feel hurt...
CUZ...
...GIVING YOU A GOOD-LUCK CHARM IS LIKE I'M ASSUMING YOU'LL BE IN DANGER.
Charms to ward off evil exist because the evil really causes disasters!
YOU DON'T NEED...
...A GOOD-LUCK CHARM...

...CUZ YOU...
...WON'T BE IN DANGER...
YOU'RE RIGHT...
Heh
...
UM...
...BUT...
... PLEASE DO BE CARE-FUL...
...JUST IN CASE...
...
I WILL.
BUT I WON'T GET HURT.
Phew...
NO...

KYOKO.
AH...
I have to go now...
EXCUSE ME... THAT'S WHAT I CAME TO SEE YOU ABOUT.
Okay.
...BUT I ENDED UP MAKING YOU COME HERE AS WELL.
NO.
DON'T WORRY.
I'm fine.
YOU DO YOUR BEST WITH YOUR SHOOT.
I will!
GOOD-BYE.
bow

YOU DON'T NEED A GOOD-LUCK CHARM...
...CUZ YOU...
...WON'T BE IN DANGER ...

...
I WONDER ABOUT THAT BLUNT-FORCE REASONING ...
shake shake
I COULDN'T HELP THINKING "WHAT SHOULD I DO WITH THIS GIRL?"...
SHE'S RIGHT.
...MORE THAN IF SHE'D JUST GIVEN ME THE GOOD-LUCK CHARM AND SAID SHE WAS WORRIED.
tmp
tmp
I ALMOST BROKE OUT INTO A SMILE AND REACHED FOR HER.
He was already smiling though.
THE PRESIDENT HAS HER WITH ME AS MY GOOD-LUCK CHARM...
... BECAUSE HE HAS HIS "REASONS."
Like food.
And food.
And food.
And food.
tmp tmp tmp tmp
CUZ...
...GIVING YOU A GOOD-LUCK CHARM IS LIKE I'M ASSUMING YOU'D BE IN DANGER.
THAT GIRL ...
... WARDS OFF EVIL.

WHEN YOU'RE STUCK AND CAN'T FREE YOURSELF...

...SHE'S THE GOOD-LUCK CHARM...

... WHO'LL SAVE YOU.

SHE'S THE STRONGEST GOOD-LUCK CHARM AVAILABLE.

...
WHEN HE SAID THAT...
I THOUGHT HE WAS BLOWING THINGS OUT OF PROPORTION...
...IN REGARDS TO MY EATING AND ABOUT HIDING THE IDENTITY OF CAIN HEEL.
I DIDN'T WORRY TOO MUCH BECAUSE HE ALWAYS GOES OVERBOARD ABOUT EVERY-THING.

...LIKE I'M ASSUMING YOU'D BE IN DANGER.
...HAVE SOME OTHER REASON IN MIND?
SOME-THING WRONG ?
BUT DID...
...THE PRESI-DENT...
UH...
grab

End of Act 163

Skip-Beat! End Notes

Everyone knows how to be a fan, but sometimes cool things from other cultures need a little help crossing the language barrier.

Page 363, panel 1: 700,000 yen
About $9,000 U.S.

Page 457, panel 1: Blood type B
In Japan, blood type is often linked to personality traits. Type B personalities are passionate and creative.

Page 477, panel 8: Yukata
A casual type of kimono usually made of cotton. Often provided at Japanese inns.

Page 515, panel 5: Carnivorous
In Japan, "herbivores" has recently come to refer to people who have no interest in a romantic relationship, or are very passive about trying to get a romantic partner. In contrast, "carnivores" actively seek out someone.

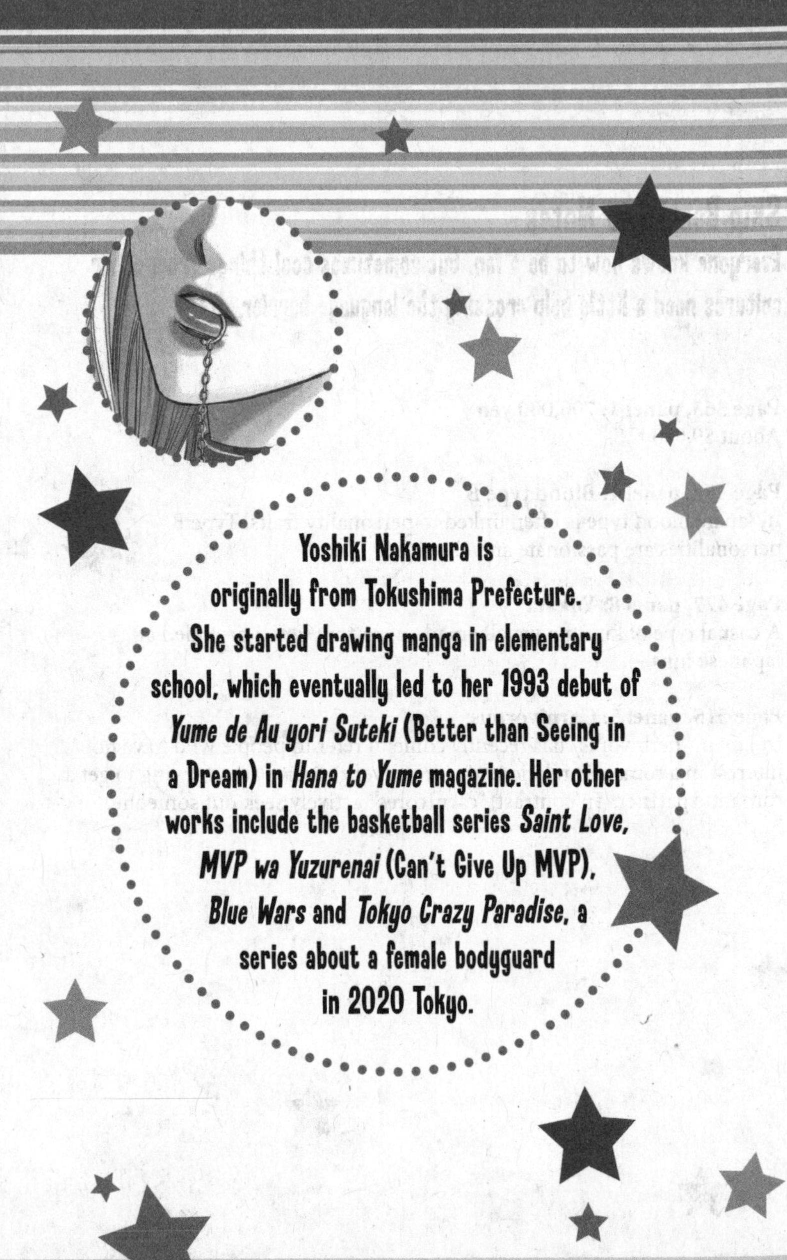

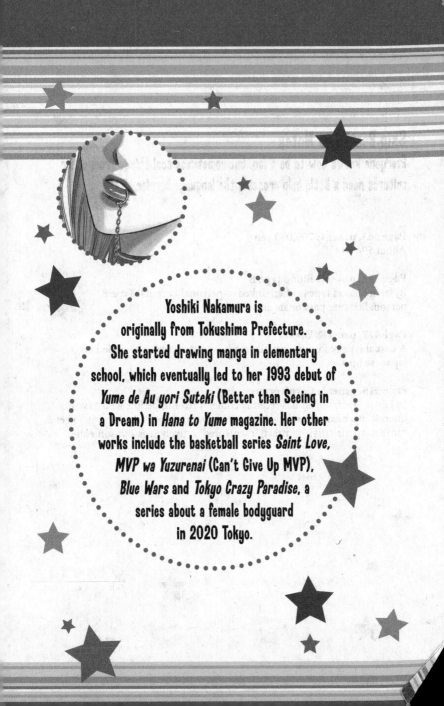

Yoshiki Nakamura is originally from Tokushima Prefecture. She started drawing manga in elementary school, which eventually led to her 1993 debut of *Yume de Au yori Suteki* (Better than Seeing in a Dream) in *Hana to Yume* magazine. Her other works include the basketball series *Saint Love, MVP wa Yuzurenai* (Can't Give Up MVP), *Blue Wars* and *Tokyo Crazy Paradise*, a series about a female bodyguard in 2020 Tokyo.

SKIP·BEAT!
3-in-1 Edition
Vol. 9

A compilation of graphic novel volumes 25-27

STORY AND ART BY YOSHIKI NAKAMURA

English Translation & Adaptation/Tomo Kimura
Touch-up Art & Lettering/Sabrina Heep
Design/Yukiko Whitley
Editor/Pancha Diaz

First published in Japan in 2010, 2011 by HAKUSENSHA, Inc., Tokyo.
English language translation rights arranged with HAKUSENSHA, Inc., Tokyo.

Printed in the U.S.A.

Published by VIZ Media, LLC
P.O. Box 77010
San Francisco, CA 94107

www.viz.com

www.shojobeat.com

10 9 8 7 6 5 4 3 2 1
3-in-1 edition first printing, November 2014

PARENTAL ADVISORY
SKIP·BEAT! is rated T for Teen and is recommended for ages 13 and up. This volume contains a grudge.
ratings.viz.com